# Building a Culture of Literacy Month-by-Month

## Hilarie B. Davis
### Illustrations by Larry Ross

EYE ON EDUCATION
6 DEPOT WAY WEST, SUITE 106
LARCHMONT, NY 10538
(914) 833-0551
(914) 833-0761 fax
www.eyeoneducation.com

Library of Congress Cataloging-in-Publication Data

Davis, Hilarie B.
  Building a culture of literacy month-by-month / Hilarie B. Davis ; illustrations by Larry Ross.
     p. cm.
  ISBN 978-1-59667-067-9
  1. English language—Study and teaching—Activity programs.
2. Calendar. I. Title.
  LB1576.D23727 2007
  372.6—dc22

2007029850

10 9 8 7 6 5 4 3 2 1

Editorial and production services provided by
Hypertext Book and Journal Services
738 Saltillo St., San Antonio, TX 78207-6953 (210-227-6055)

## Also Available from EYE ON EDUCATION

**Family Reading Night**
Darcy J. Hutchins, Marsha D. Greenfield, and Joyce L. Epstein

**Active Literacy Across the Curriculum:**
**Strategies for Reading, Writing, Speaking, and Listening**
Heidi Hayes Jacobs

**But I'm Not a Reading Teacher:**
**Strategies for Literacy Instruction in the Content Areas**
Amy Benjamin

**Writing in the Content Areas, 2nd Edition**
Amy Benjamin

**Writing Put to the Test: Teaching for the High-Stakes Essay**
Amy Benjamin

**Differentiated Instruction: A Guide for Elementary Teachers**
Amy Benjamin

**Literature Circles That Engage Middle and High School Students**
Victor and Marc Moeller

**Socratic Seminars and Literature Circles for**
**Middle and High School English**
Victor and Marc Moeller

**What Great Teachers Do Differently:**
**14 Things that Matter Most**
Todd Whitaker

**Seven Simple Secrets: What the Best Teachers Know and Do**
Annette Breaux and Todd Whitaker

**Classroom Motivation From A to Z:**
**How to Engage Your Students in Learning**
Barbara Blackburn

**Classroom Instruction From A to Z:**
**How to Promote Student Learning**
Barbara Blackburn

*This book is dedicated to my wise and patient husband—*
*my first and best supporter and critic.*

# Meet the Author

A former teacher, Hilarie B. Davis is the president and chief executive officer of Technology for Learning Consortium, Inc. She specializes in developing, supporting, and evaluating student-centered learning environments.

This book was inspired in part by her work with the urban Pennsylvania Harrisburg School District under the leadership of Dr. Gerald Kohn and with the Native American Lower Brule School District under the leadership of Bill Williams and Bob Foudray. She has worked with these and other school districts to develop a culture of literacy.

With a doctoral degree from the University of Rochester, Hilarie has also served as the director of curriculum and instruction for the Madison School District in New Jersey, adjunct faculty member at Johnson and Wales University, and researcher at the federally funded Lab at Brown University.

She also served as vice president of curriculum and instruction for Optical Data Corporation where she shepherded the development and implementation of the first multimedia program to compete successfully with elementary science textbooks. She also produced a film documentary about a literacy program which had been implemented in New York City's District 2.

Her workshops and professional development presentations focus on a wide array of topics which include: building a culture of literacy, the questioning reader, teaching and learning in the information age, and higher level thinking for students and teachers.

Hilarie is an avid reader, from science fiction to historical fiction to social commentary, and lives with her husband Brad in Rhode Island.

# Table of Contents

**Part 1** . . . . . . . . . . . . . . . . . . . . . . . . . . . . . . . . . . . . . . . . . . . . . . . . . . . **1**

**Chapter 1. Month-by-Month Activities: An Overview** . . . . . . . . . . . . . . . **9**
Theme . . . . . . . . . . . . . . . . . . . . . . . . . . . . . . . . . . . . . . . . . . . . . . . . . . 9
Schoolwide Reading Book of the Month . . . . . . . . . . . . . . . . . . . . . . . . 10
Writing Contest . . . . . . . . . . . . . . . . . . . . . . . . . . . . . . . . . . . . . . . . . . 11
In the Halls … (Shared Knowledge-Building Activities,
    Kiosk Ideas) . . . . . . . . . . . . . . . . . . . . . . . . . . . . . . . . . . . . . . . . 12
Inspirational Highlights . . . . . . . . . . . . . . . . . . . . . . . . . . . . . . . . . . . . 13
Family Nights . . . . . . . . . . . . . . . . . . . . . . . . . . . . . . . . . . . . . . . . . . . 14
Your Plan Book for Building a Culture of Literacy . . . . . . . . . . . . . . . 14
Month-by-Month Listing of Activities . . . . . . . . . . . . . . . . . . . . . . . . . 15

**Chapter 2. August: Getting Ready to Learn** . . . . . . . . . . . . . . . . . . . . . . 17
Book of the Month . . . . . . . . . . . . . . . . . . . . . . . . . . . . . . . . . . . . . . . . 17
In the Halls … (Shared Knowledge-Building Activities) . . . . . . . . . . . 18
Share Readers' and Writers' Recommendations . . . . . . . . . . . . . . . . . . 19
Inspirational Highlights . . . . . . . . . . . . . . . . . . . . . . . . . . . . . . . . . . . . 19
Writing Contest: Goal-Setting and the Quest . . . . . . . . . . . . . . . . . . . . 20
Family Night: Talking About What You Read . . . . . . . . . . . . . . . . . . . 21
August Writing Contest . . . . . . . . . . . . . . . . . . . . . . . . . . . . . . . . . . . . 22
Family Night . . . . . . . . . . . . . . . . . . . . . . . . . . . . . . . . . . . . . . . . . . . . 23

**Chapter 3. September: Becoming a Learning Community** . . . . . . . . . . . 25
Rights and Responsibilities . . . . . . . . . . . . . . . . . . . . . . . . . . . . . . . . . 25
Book of the Month . . . . . . . . . . . . . . . . . . . . . . . . . . . . . . . . . . . . . . . . 27
In the Halls … Figurative Language . . . . . . . . . . . . . . . . . . . . . . . . . . 28
Share Readers' and Writers' Recommendations . . . . . . . . . . . . . . . . . . 29
Inspirational Highlights . . . . . . . . . . . . . . . . . . . . . . . . . . . . . . . . . . . . 30
Writing Contest: A Sense of Community, Descriptive Writing . . . . . . . 30
Family Night: Reading Together . . . . . . . . . . . . . . . . . . . . . . . . . . . . . . 32
September Writing Contest . . . . . . . . . . . . . . . . . . . . . . . . . . . . . . . . . . 33
Family Night . . . . . . . . . . . . . . . . . . . . . . . . . . . . . . . . . . . . . . . . . . . . 34

**Chapter 4. October: Beginning Where You Are** . . . . . . . . . . . . . . . . . . . 35
Book of the Month . . . . . . . . . . . . . . . . . . . . . . . . . . . . . . . . . . . . . . . . 35

In the Halls ... Segues—Words That Signal
   Text Structure and Connections . . . . . . . . . . . . . . . . . . . . . . . . . . . 36
Share Readers' and Writers' Recommendations . . . . . . . . . . . . . . . . . 37
Inspirational Highlights . . . . . . . . . . . . . . . . . . . . . . . . . . . . . . . . . . . 37
Writing Contest: Journeys, Time Sequence, Autobiography . . . . . . . . 38
Family Night: Reading to Each Other . . . . . . . . . . . . . . . . . . . . . . . . 38
October Writing Contest . . . . . . . . . . . . . . . . . . . . . . . . . . . . . . . . . . 39
Family Night . . . . . . . . . . . . . . . . . . . . . . . . . . . . . . . . . . . . . . . . . . . 40

**Chapter 5. November: Becoming Authors** . . . . . . . . . . . . . . . . . . . . . **41**
Book of the Month . . . . . . . . . . . . . . . . . . . . . . . . . . . . . . . . . . . . . . . 41
In the Halls ... Painting Pictures With Words . . . . . . . . . . . . . . . . . 42
Share Readers' and Writers' Recommendations . . . . . . . . . . . . . . . . . 43
Inspirational Highlights . . . . . . . . . . . . . . . . . . . . . . . . . . . . . . . . . . . 43
Writing Contest: Poetry . . . . . . . . . . . . . . . . . . . . . . . . . . . . . . . . . . . 44
Family Night: Interpreting What You Read . . . . . . . . . . . . . . . . . . . . 44
November Writing Contest . . . . . . . . . . . . . . . . . . . . . . . . . . . . . . . . 46
Family Night . . . . . . . . . . . . . . . . . . . . . . . . . . . . . . . . . . . . . . . . . . . 47

**Chapter 6. December: The Gift of Reading** . . . . . . . . . . . . . . . . . . . . **49**
Book of the Month . . . . . . . . . . . . . . . . . . . . . . . . . . . . . . . . . . . . . . . 49
In the Halls... Alike Or Different . . . . . . . . . . . . . . . . . . . . . . . . . . . 50
Share Readers' and Writers' Recommendations . . . . . . . . . . . . . . . . . 51
Inspirational Highlights . . . . . . . . . . . . . . . . . . . . . . . . . . . . . . . . . . . 51
Writing Contest: Book Reviews, Compare/Contrast . . . . . . . . . . . . . 51
Family Night: Poetry for Dessert . . . . . . . . . . . . . . . . . . . . . . . . . . . . 52
December Writing Contest . . . . . . . . . . . . . . . . . . . . . . . . . . . . . . . . 53
Family Night . . . . . . . . . . . . . . . . . . . . . . . . . . . . . . . . . . . . . . . . . . . 54

**Chapter 7. January: Celebrating Progress** . . . . . . . . . . . . . . . . . . . . . **55**
Book of the Month . . . . . . . . . . . . . . . . . . . . . . . . . . . . . . . . . . . . . . . 55
In the Halls ... Plotting With Seven Basic Plots . . . . . . . . . . . . . . . . . 56
Share Readers' and Writers' Recommendations . . . . . . . . . . . . . . . . . 57
Inspirational Highlights . . . . . . . . . . . . . . . . . . . . . . . . . . . . . . . . . . . 57
Writing Contest: Celebrating Progress, Problem and Solution . . . . . . 58
Family Night: Grandparents as Storyteller . . . . . . . . . . . . . . . . . . . . 58
January Writing Contest . . . . . . . . . . . . . . . . . . . . . . . . . . . . . . . . . . 59
Family Night . . . . . . . . . . . . . . . . . . . . . . . . . . . . . . . . . . . . . . . . . . . 60

**Chapter 8. February: Speaking and Listening** . . . . . . . . . . . . . . . . . . **61**
Book of the Month . . . . . . . . . . . . . . . . . . . . . . . . . . . . . . . . . . . . . . . 61

In the Halls … Flights of Fantasy .................................. 62
Share Readers' and Writers' Recommendations .................... 62
Inspirational Highlights ................................... 63
Writing Contest: Fantasy .................................... 63
Family Night: Favorites .................................... 64
February Writing Contest .................................... 65
Family Night .................................................. 66

**Chapter 9. March: Reading to Learn, Writing to Understand** ......... 67
Book of the Month .......................................... 67
In the Halls … Cause and Effect ............................. 68
Share Readers' and Writers' Recommendations .................... 69
Inspirational Highlights ................................... 69
Writing Contest: Folktales, Cause and Effect .................... 70
Family Night: Improvisation ................................ 71
March Writing Contest ...................................... 72
Family Night .................................................. 73

**Chapter 10. April: Writing to Communicate Feelings and Ideas** ....... 75
Book of the Month .......................................... 75
In the Halls … Caught in the Middle ........................... 76
Share Readers' and Writers' Recommendations .................... 77
Inspirational Highlights ................................... 77
Writing Contest: Illustrated Short Story About Feelings ............. 78
Family Night: Art in Literature ............................. 79
April Writing Contest ...................................... 80
Family Night .................................................. 81

**Chapter 11. May: Weaving Our Stories Together** ................... 83
Book of the Month .......................................... 83
In the Halls … Nonfiction .................................. 84
Share Readers' and Writers' Recommendations .................... 84
Inspirational Highlights ................................... 84
Writing Contest: Partnerships, Nonfiction ...................... 85
Family Night: Reading to Learn ............................. 86
May Writing Contest ........................................ 87
Family Night .................................................. 88

**Chapter 12. June and July: Read On** ............................ 89
Book of the Month .......................................... 89
In the Halls … Illusions, Allusions, Foreshadowing and Mystery .... 90
Share Readers' and Writers' Recommendations .................... 90

Inspirational Highlights . . . . . . . . . . . . . . . . . . . . . . . . . . . . . . . . . . . . 90
Writing Contest: Read on, Mystery . . . . . . . . . . . . . . . . . . . . . . . . . 91
Summer Writing Contest . . . . . . . . . . . . . . . . . . . . . . . . . . . . . . . . . . . 92
Final Reflection . . . . . . . . . . . . . . . . . . . . . . . . . . . . . . . . . . . . . . . . . . . 93

**Part 2: Study Guide** . . . . . . . . . . . . . . . . . . . . . . . . . . . . . . . . . . . . . **106**

**Chapter 13. How Do You Start Telling the Story of Your School?** . . . . . . **107**
Story Starters . . . . . . . . . . . . . . . . . . . . . . . . . . . . . . . . . . . . . . . . . . . . 108
Tell the Community's Stories . . . . . . . . . . . . . . . . . . . . . . . . . . . . . . 109
Spread the Word . . . . . . . . . . . . . . . . . . . . . . . . . . . . . . . . . . . . . . . . . 110
Monthly Writing Contest . . . . . . . . . . . . . . . . . . . . . . . . . . . . . . . . . 110
Lunchtime Literacy Activities . . . . . . . . . . . . . . . . . . . . . . . . . . . . . 111
March Writing Contest . . . . . . . . . . . . . . . . . . . . . . . . . . . . . . . . . . . 111
What Makes My Writing Worth Reading? Writer's Rubric . . . . . . . . . 112
Stories About Learning to Read . . . . . . . . . . . . . . . . . . . . . . . . . . . 113

**Chapter 14. What is a Culture of Literacy?** . . . . . . . . . . . . . . . . . . . . . **115**
Books, Books and More Books . . . . . . . . . . . . . . . . . . . . . . . . . . . . 116
Language is Fun . . . . . . . . . . . . . . . . . . . . . . . . . . . . . . . . . . . . . . . . . 116
Language is Productive . . . . . . . . . . . . . . . . . . . . . . . . . . . . . . . . . . . 116
Using Language Well is Everyone's Right and Responsibility . . . . . . 117
Student Rights and Responsibilities . . . . . . . . . . . . . . . . . . . . . . . . 117
Teacher Rights and Responsibilities . . . . . . . . . . . . . . . . . . . . . . . . 119
Administrator Rights and Responsibilities . . . . . . . . . . . . . . . . . . 120
Family/Caregiver Rights and Responsibilities . . . . . . . . . . . . . . . 121

**Chapter 15. How Does Language Work?** . . . . . . . . . . . . . . . . . . . . . . . . **125**
Children are "Hardwired" to Learn Language . . . . . . . . . . . . . . . . 126
English Does Not Always Follow the Rules . . . . . . . . . . . . . . . . . . 126
Written English is Made Up of Five Basic Elements . . . . . . . . . . . . 126
Letters and Sounds . . . . . . . . . . . . . . . . . . . . . . . . . . . . . . . . . . . . . . 127
Four Types of Sentences . . . . . . . . . . . . . . . . . . . . . . . . . . . . . . . . . . 127
Seven Types of Paragraphs . . . . . . . . . . . . . . . . . . . . . . . . . . . . . . . 128
Texts: Fiction and Nonfiction . . . . . . . . . . . . . . . . . . . . . . . . . . . . . 129
Seven Basic Plots . . . . . . . . . . . . . . . . . . . . . . . . . . . . . . . . . . . . . . . . 130
Six Nonfiction or Informational Organizations . . . . . . . . . . . . . . . . 131
Genres . . . . . . . . . . . . . . . . . . . . . . . . . . . . . . . . . . . . . . . . . . . . . . . . . 132
Reading is All About the Cues . . . . . . . . . . . . . . . . . . . . . . . . . . . . . 132
Encourage Students to Start Stories . . . . . . . . . . . . . . . . . . . . . . . . 133
Post Story Ideas . . . . . . . . . . . . . . . . . . . . . . . . . . . . . . . . . . . . . . . . . 135

**Chapter 16. What Does it Mean to Be Literate?** . . . . . . . . . . . . . . . . . . . . . **139**
Literate Students Are Strategic . . . . . . . . . . . . . . . . . . . . . . . . . . . . . . . . 140
Literate Students Are Ready to Learn . . . . . . . . . . . . . . . . . . . . . . . . . . 140
Literate Students Are Able to Reflect . . . . . . . . . . . . . . . . . . . . . . . . . . 140
Literate Students Are Confident . . . . . . . . . . . . . . . . . . . . . . . . . . . . . . 142
Literate Students Develop Knowledge and Skills Through
    Reading and Writing . . . . . . . . . . . . . . . . . . . . . . . . . . . . . . . . . . . . 142
Teacher Favorites . . . . . . . . . . . . . . . . . . . . . . . . . . . . . . . . . . . . . . . . . . 143
Student Favorites . . . . . . . . . . . . . . . . . . . . . . . . . . . . . . . . . . . . . . . . . . 144

**Chapter 17. How Does a Culture of Literacy Develop Among
Teachers in a School?** . . . . . . . . . . . . . . . . . . . . . . . . . . . . . . . . . . . **145**
Build a Vision Together . . . . . . . . . . . . . . . . . . . . . . . . . . . . . . . . . . . . . 145
Use Data to Open Up Discussions . . . . . . . . . . . . . . . . . . . . . . . . . . . . 147
Understanding Literacy Development . . . . . . . . . . . . . . . . . . . . . . . . . 148
Letters . . . . . . . . . . . . . . . . . . . . . . . . . . . . . . . . . . . . . . . . . . . . . . . . . . . . 149
Words . . . . . . . . . . . . . . . . . . . . . . . . . . . . . . . . . . . . . . . . . . . . . . . . . . . . . 150
Sentences . . . . . . . . . . . . . . . . . . . . . . . . . . . . . . . . . . . . . . . . . . . . . . . . . 153
Paragraphs . . . . . . . . . . . . . . . . . . . . . . . . . . . . . . . . . . . . . . . . . . . . . . . 155
Texts: Fiction and Nonfiction . . . . . . . . . . . . . . . . . . . . . . . . . . . . . . . . 157
Make the Continuum a Living, Working Tool . . . . . . . . . . . . . . . . . . 159
Share the Continuum With Students and Their Families . . . . . . . . . . 160

**Chapter 18. What Do You See in a Classroom Devoted to
Literacy Development?** . . . . . . . . . . . . . . . . . . . . . . . . . . . . . . . . . . . **163**
Planning . . . . . . . . . . . . . . . . . . . . . . . . . . . . . . . . . . . . . . . . . . . . . . . . . . 164
Use of Time . . . . . . . . . . . . . . . . . . . . . . . . . . . . . . . . . . . . . . . . . . . . . . . 166
Focus . . . . . . . . . . . . . . . . . . . . . . . . . . . . . . . . . . . . . . . . . . . . . . . . . . . . . 173
Instruction . . . . . . . . . . . . . . . . . . . . . . . . . . . . . . . . . . . . . . . . . . . . . . . . 175
Assessment . . . . . . . . . . . . . . . . . . . . . . . . . . . . . . . . . . . . . . . . . . . . . . . 178

**Chapter 19. How Do You Involve Families and the Community?** . . . . . **185**
Read to Each Other . . . . . . . . . . . . . . . . . . . . . . . . . . . . . . . . . . . . . . . . . 186
Read Together . . . . . . . . . . . . . . . . . . . . . . . . . . . . . . . . . . . . . . . . . . . . . 187
Talk About What You Read . . . . . . . . . . . . . . . . . . . . . . . . . . . . . . . . . . 188
Art and Literature . . . . . . . . . . . . . . . . . . . . . . . . . . . . . . . . . . . . . . . . . . 189
Improvisation . . . . . . . . . . . . . . . . . . . . . . . . . . . . . . . . . . . . . . . . . . . . . . 189
Quiz Show Night . . . . . . . . . . . . . . . . . . . . . . . . . . . . . . . . . . . . . . . . . . . 189
Favorites . . . . . . . . . . . . . . . . . . . . . . . . . . . . . . . . . . . . . . . . . . . . . . . . . . 190
Poetry for Dessert . . . . . . . . . . . . . . . . . . . . . . . . . . . . . . . . . . . . . . . . . . 190
Grandparents as Storytellers . . . . . . . . . . . . . . . . . . . . . . . . . . . . . . . . . 191
Business Partners . . . . . . . . . . . . . . . . . . . . . . . . . . . . . . . . . . . . . . . . . . . 192

Community Organizations as Partners
(Informal, Faith-Based, Service) . . . . . . . . . . . . . . . . . . . . . . . . . . 192

**Chapter 20. How Do You Immerse Students in Literacy Through
What They See and Hear Every Day?** . . . . . . . . . . . . . . . . . . . . . . **195**
Meet a Reader, Writer, or Thinker . . . . . . . . . . . . . . . . . . . . . . . . . . 196
Every Day Message on Chart Paper . . . . . . . . . . . . . . . . . . . . . . . . . 196
Post Visuals of What is Important . . . . . . . . . . . . . . . . . . . . . . . . . . 198
Story Map the Book of the Month . . . . . . . . . . . . . . . . . . . . . . . . . . 199
Read Aloud in Morning Announcements . . . . . . . . . . . . . . . . . . . . . 201
Read With Students . . . . . . . . . . . . . . . . . . . . . . . . . . . . . . . . . . . . 201

**Chapter 21. How Do You Celebrate Speaking and Listening?** . . . . . . . . **203**
Talk About Your Own Reading and Writing . . . . . . . . . . . . . . . . . . . 203
Feature Student Authors . . . . . . . . . . . . . . . . . . . . . . . . . . . . . . . . . 204
Feature Teacher Authors . . . . . . . . . . . . . . . . . . . . . . . . . . . . . . . . . 205
Find the Writers in Your Community . . . . . . . . . . . . . . . . . . . . . . . . 205
Interview Students . . . . . . . . . . . . . . . . . . . . . . . . . . . . . . . . . . . . . 207
Emphasize Learning as a Continuum . . . . . . . . . . . . . . . . . . . . . . . . 208
Expect Everyone to Speak Respectfully . . . . . . . . . . . . . . . . . . . . . . 208
Put Literacy Into the School Schedule . . . . . . . . . . . . . . . . . . . . . . . 208

**Conclusion** . . . . . . . . . . . . . . . . . . . . . . . . . . . . . . . . . . . . . . . . . . . **211**

# Introduction to Part 1

When a whole school decides to help children develop as readers and writers, everyone has a role. In every way, through many small actions, adults and children begin to pay attention to their own and others' use of language. From talking about what they are reading and writing, to helping each other with difficulties, from sharing favorite books to talking about interesting words—the whole community becomes intensely interested in language. At a very basic level, everyone already knows what research tells us: that children who read more read better, and that being able to read means you are more likely to be successful in life and to contribute to society.

> *The principles and monthly activities are designed to keep your feet firmly on the ground, your heart open to the community you serve, and your vision clearly in mind.*

A literacy leader can be the principal, literacy facilitator, or reading teacher who sets the tone for collaborative learning and nurtures the culture that sustains it. He/she can bring people together, make connections that move things along, actively support each individual who gets involved, and spark conversations that result in even more involvement. Everyone is *for* children learning to read, so it is already a shared goal of teachers, children, and families. What *is* needed is leadership that makes it the norm to talk about how children are doing in relationship to the environment created by the adults. That leader gives makes everyone a part of the problem AND part of the solution, giving them permission to learn and to change. This book is about how to rally the well-meaning people in your school around helping every child to read and write well.

If you are a leader in a school whose students are looking to lift off as readers and writers, this book is for you. The effort you put into being the leader—cheerleader, ringleader, bandleader, and coach—will create ability. But just as important, it will focus effort and build excitement to develop the confidence to pay close attention to how each child is learning to read and write, and how each interaction supports the goal of having every single child read and write with joy and ease.

*How is the book organized?* This book is organized the way your life as a school leader is organized—around the activities that you do every day. It provides practical activities and inspiration to be more creative and effective.

The first section provides month-by-month activities based on the principles in the study guide that follows. In the study guide you will learn how to create a culture of literacy through emphasizing story, defining a culture of literacy, unlocking the secrets of how language works, building an understanding of what it means to literate, involving families, creating a community of practice, giving and taking feedback, using the physical environment to immerse students in literacy, and celebrating speaking and listening. You can start by dipping into the months, or reading about the principles, or you can use them together as you move through the year. A plan book is provided in the middle of the book for you to add ideas, note what works for you, and jot down ideas for next year. You may even decide to use the study guide chapters for monthly faculty meetings.

*What this book offers you?* This book combines theory and practice to suggest ways to think and things to try to make language important to children and to empower them to use what they know as speakers of the language to read and write it. You will find ideas for working with teachers and for being the instructional leader that you are so everyone sees you as walking the talk that language development is central. You can be the symbolic and practical leader of literacy in your building. By adopting the principles and practices described here, you will be perceived as an active and knowledgeable leader who provides continuity and inspiration. The activities are simple, practical, and powerful so you can do them easily within your normal day. The principles and monthly activities are designed to keep your feet firmly on the ground, your heart open to the community you serve, and your vision clearly in mind. This book anchors what is known about literacy in activities you do every day.

## Introduction: *What is Culture?*

Culture is a way of life for a group of people based on the behaviors, beliefs, values, and symbols they accept. It is the stories we tell ourselves about how best to live our lives. Culture is shaped through social interaction among the people of a group as they discuss what they think ought to be done, the decision-making process, and navigation of different ideas. A culture develops rules, roles, and rituals that work well enough to be considered valid as a way to perceive, think, and feel. *At least for awhile.* What is needed is to make the culture part of the conversation so you are continually revisiting the underlying assumptions to inquire whether they are still useful. As people grow together, new rituals develop, rules are retired, and different people take on familiar roles.

The culture of a group is revealed in its rules, roles, rituals, symbols, objects, language, and space. You can figure out the culture of a place by looking at these areas. Oftentimes, the culture is invisible to the people within it because it is all they know. When a school is unable to meet its goals, sometimes it is because facets of the culture are not consistent with the goals. They keep wondering why they are not getting further along, when they are being held back by a set of common, unexamined behaviors. By examining your school's culture, you will be able to make what you are doing explicit to help every child learn to read and write well, and identify what you are doing that may not serve that goal.

What do your objects, symbols, language, rules, roles, and rituals reveal about how your school views literacy development? How can you consciously create a culture of literacy? In this book, you will look at the facets of your culture and consider options for making them more strongly support literacy.

## Rules

A culture develops rules about what is good and bad, worthy and worthless, and right and wrong. For example, "finish your worksheets" is a rule in some schools that value task completion, while in other schools, "always have a good book to read" is a rule because they value reading. While finishing tasks is important, rules that emphasize finishing rather than learning shift the focus of the culture away from literacy. Think about some of the rules in your school that would be invoked to answer these questions:

- What are students expected to read? To write?
- How much of the time are students talking to each other about their reading and writing?
- What kinds of reading materials are available and valued?
- How do students learn thinking and learning strategies?
- How much are teachers and students expected to know about what students know and can do with language?
- What is important to teach?

## Roles

A culture also defines people's roles based on who and what is valued. For example, if the teacher is the only one who reads aloud, the message is that she is the only one who can serve as a role model for good reading. When students read aloud to each other, make tapes of their reading so others can listen, read aloud to younger children and read aloud to their parents, the message from the culture is that reading aloud is an everyday, really nice form of language that everyone can share by reading or listening. When students are both readers and listeners, they become better at both roles.

Having students read aloud during morning announcements, at family nights, and during morning activities in the classroom help to create a culture of a rich, oral-language culture in which they have an important role. Think about the roles in your building:

- ◆ Who reads what?
- ◆ Who reads to whom? When? Why?
- ◆ Who gets published?

## Rituals

Every culture has rituals or ways things are done, like taking roll, making morning announcements, walking to specials, having parents involved in school, and how students relate to one another. These rituals make everyday things routine and send important messages about what is important. For example, are your students asked to walk single file in a straight line without speaking on the way to specials or lunch? Are they able to? In some schools, this ritual is positive and is done with pride. Students see it as a time of transition and quiet between activities. In others, both students and teachers struggle with it. It may be that in these schools, students need to walk together in small groups, conversing about things that interest them on the way to specials, or they may need to walk in a straight line without talking. The goal can be to "converse quietly with your classmates as you walk between classes" or "take this time to think about what you were just doing and what you will be doing next" or "make this a quiet time and walk in single file." When rituals are difficult to enforce there may very well may be a disconnect between the culture and the stated goals. Making the ritual about the goal, rather than against the behavior, builds the culture toward the goal. What do the rituals in your school reveal?

- ◆ Announcements: Who makes schoolwide announcements? When are they made? How do they begin? "May I have your attention?" or "Please excuse the interruption."
- ◆ Celebrations: What is celebrated? Progress, participation, excellence? How is it celebrated? Who identifies what is worth celebrating? Who is consistently celebrated?

- Rewards: Is good behavior rewarded? What is good behavior? Who defines it? Is creativity rewarded? Who defines the rewards? Who delivers them? Are they intrinsic or extrinsic?

- Principal activities: What do students see the principal doing? Caring about? What would the students say the principal thinks about reading and writing?

- Family nights: How do families find out about them? What language are the announcements sent home in? Do families do things together at family nights? Do parents have input into family nights? Are there literacy activities at these events?

- Lunchtime activities: What do students do when they are waiting for lunch? After they have eaten? Do they have options? Are they encouraged to converse or share ideas and interests? Are there interested adults to converse with them? Are there monitors who remind them of the rules?

## Symbols and Space

These are the tangible manifestations of culture. Some symbols are so important that they are protected by law, such as a country's flag. Remember the alphabet over the chalkboard in your kindergarten classroom? It was posted as a practical matter but it was also a symbol of how important those letters were to your development. Symbols are words, gestures, pictures, or objects that carry a particular meaning developed by a culture. Some objects take on a life of their own—the rocking chair the librarian sits in to read is a symbol of someone sharing a story.

- Does your school have a symbol?
- What is your school known for?
- Do you have a school or learning pledge to open the day or each class?
- What best symbolizes your school's commitment to literacy?

Think about all the monuments, plaques, and sculptures in carefully designed public spaces. They are designed to reflect the values of the politicians, and to influence those who enter those spaces. How space is organized sends important messages about what a culture values. When you walk through your school, what do the spaces tell people about what you value in literacy?

- What does your building reveal about how you view literacy?
- Where are the books in your building?
- What does the foyer say? Make the foyer say "think big!"
- What does the principal's office say? Make the principal's office say "wonder!"
- What does the library say? Make the library say "share what *you* are writing!"
- What do the halls say? Make the halls say "ask someone what they think!"
- What do the classrooms say? Make the classrooms say "talk about what you read, write, and think!"
- What does the cafeteria say? Make the cafeteria say "share your interests!"

## Language

Language is a critical factor in culture. Through language, people signal formality or informality, convey acceptance or rejection, develop inside jokes, and create a shared history. Songs, mottos, and sayings develop in a culture as ways people talk to each other and to themselves. In a culture of literacy, people use encouraging words about any effort at reading and writing. They talk about the effort they are putting into writing as a puzzle to be solved, and express excitement about the ideas they are thinking through. They expect to be successful and enjoy the process.

When you think about the language in your school, consider what percentage of the talk sounds like this.

- How much of the talk you overhear, listen into in lessons, or catch in the classroom when students are working independently shows genuine interest in reading and writing?
- Consider the qualities of the talk you hear. Is it honest, positive and interesting? Or is it more routine and superficial?
- What kind of language do students and teachers use? Is the tone casual and warm, formal and businesslike, respectful, playful, or curious? What do you want it to be?

## Summary

Culture is a way of life based on social interactions, the development of rules, roles, and rituals, symbols to define intentions and importance, spaces that reveal values, and language that shapes interactions, intentions, and understandings. Your school is a reflection of everyone from the youngest to the oldest and its culture is revealed through actions and words. When the culture reflects the values and beliefs then the two are aligned and literacy can take hold.

What do your objects, symbols, language, rules, roles, and rituals reveal about your school culture? How can you consciously create your schools culture? The answers to these questions lie in your ability to shape and understand your current environment and bring forward the positives and replace the negatives. Consider the established rules. Do they reflect the cultural expectations and goals and encourage rather than threaten or direct? What roles do the members of your community play in allowing for and encouraging the growth of literacy? Do your teachers read to the students? Do the students read to the teachers? Do they read for understanding and growth? What rituals do you and the others in your school community perform? Every culture has rituals or ways of doing things, like taking roll, making morning announcements, walking to specials, having parents involved in school, and how students relate to one another. Help create and support activities that emphasize the importance of rituals and utilize them as part of an overall plan to create a culture of literacy within your school. Chose your words and actions carefully and thoughtfully as they will begin to shape your culture of literacy.

## Reflection

Through the activities in Part 1 and the background in Part 2, you can become a student of your own culture, peeling away the layers to reveal the underlying assumptions behind the rules, roles, rituals, and the messages the symbols, language, space, and objects send. By revealing the assumptions and examining the messages, you can ask how they can better serve your literacy goals.

# Chapter 1

# Month-by-Month Activities: An Overview

A culture of literacy has rules, roles, and rituals that embody what it values about literacy, learning, and teaching. Here you will find a plan book of activities based on the principles in the study guide. Every month has a core set of activities:

- ◆ Theme
- ◆ Book of the month for the whole school to read
- ◆ Writing contest
- ◆ In the halls … (shared knowledge-building activities)
- ◆ Ways to share readers' and writers' recommendations
- ◆ Inspiration from readers and writers to post on an easel each week and highlight in morning announcements

The first month of activities is August. If your year begins in September, you will want to shift the activities ahead a month since the August theme is "getting ready to learn." Regular weekly and monthly routines are described with specific activities. You will find parent letters for family nights that support the activities described in the Part 2 chapter on families. You will find suggestions for the book of the month and writing contests. A plan book for each month is provided where you can add your own ideas and customize the calendar (pages 94 through 105).

In the next couple of pages, the core set of activities are listed as an overview of the year. After the plan book pages, the activities are described in more detail by month.

## Theme

The themes were chosen by the time of year and to build on each other. To use the theme to create conversations and stimulate thinking, post it on a banner in the entryway, mention it at least once a week in morning announce-ments, and talk about it in the last faculty meeting of the previous month. Themes are a way to provide focus for everyone in the school, so students see these big ideas are important for everyone. They are a way to have discussions about big ideas and plan joint activities among faculty so they develop a stron-ger sense of the developmental continuum. The themes by month are:

- August: Getting Ready to Learn
- September: Becoming a Learning Community
- October: Beginning Where You Are
- November: Becoming Authors
- December: The Gift of Reading
- January: Celebrating Progress
- February: Speaking and Listening
- March: Reading to Learn, Writing to Understand
- April: Writing to Communicate Feelings and Ideas
- May: Weaving Our Stories Together
- June and July: Read On

## Schoolwide Reading Book of the Month

Building on the idea that it "takes a village" to raise a child, the book of the month gets children from kindergarten to sixth grade reading the same book. You will need a copy of the book for every classroom. To prepare, make the book the focus of a faculty meeting the month before so teachers can brain-storm by grade level about how they will use the book with their students. Then during the month, each class reads and responds to the book, creating responses they can post in the hall for everyone. Responses might make con-nections with their curriculum, their experience or other books. They might be books written in the style of the book of the month, or sequels, or responses to other books by the author or the genre, or anything else. It is the richness that is important to share, showing everyone that books hold mean-ing for a wide range of ages and evoke different responses. By seeing the different responses from other students throughout the school to the same book they read, the children broaden their own range of possible responses to that book and to others in the future.

- August: *Oh, the Places You'll Go!* By Dr. Seuss
- September: *Stone Soup* by Marcia Brown
- October: *Walk On! A Guide for Babies of All Ages* by Marla Frazee

- November: *Click, Clack, Moo Cows That Type* by Doreen Cronin
- December: *Wild About Books* by Judy Sierra
- January: *The Daddy Mountain* by Jules Feiffer
- February: *The Frog Princess: A Tlingit Legend from Alaska* by Eric A. Kimmel and Rosanne Litzinger
- March: *Why Mosquitoes Buzz in People's Ears* by Verna Aardema
- April: *Waiting for Gregory* by Kimberly Willis Holt
- May: *If You Give a Mouse a Cookie* by Laura Joffe Numeroff
- June and July: *Magic Beach* by Crockett Johnson

## Writing Contest

In a culture of literacy, everyone is an author. A monthly writing contest engages students as authors in several ways. It encourages students to share in the excitement of writing and being read as an author. At the same time they are developing their own ideas on a topic and within a style or genre, they get to see all the possibilities for writing about a topic from others. By having a whole-school

STARTING WRITING CONTEST

writing contest, the developmental continuum is apparent to everyone. Responses to a writing challenge at all different levels create a natural opportunity for students to learn from those just a bit beyond their skills, and to see where they have come from by looking at other's writing. Why not just post the writing of everyone as with the book of the month responses? The "contest" creates some competition with oneself and with others—healthy competition to do the best one can—and to be recognized for excellence. When you talk about the writing contest as a faculty, you may decide to de-emphasize the contest idea and instead rotate through classes or choose randomly from the ones students submit to be considered. The suggested topics and focus for each month are:

- August: Goal Setting, the Quest
- September: Community, descriptive essay
- October: Journeys, time sequence, autobiography

- November: Poetry
- December: Book reviews, compare/contrast
- January: Celebrating progress, problem and solution
- February: Fantasy
- March: Folktales, cause and effect
- April: Short story about feelings
- May: Partnerships, nonfiction
- June and July: Read on, mystery

Announce the writing contest by the first Friday of the month. Choose the best pieces for each grade level by the third Friday of the month so that student authors can be featured at the Family Night on the last Thursday of the month.

## In the Halls ... (Shared Knowledge-Building Activities, Kiosk Ideas)

Remember when you enter a culture, the space reveals a lot about the culture. By planning for formal and informal spaces for students and teachers to communicate, you create a vibrant literacy community. Every month there are suggestions for conversation starters to be posted in the halls. The chart paper that comes on the roll is perfect for this. Cut a strip of paper 10-12' long and hang horizontally, low enough for young students to write on. Post them in different hallways to provoke interest and participation. Have the faculty plan to have students contribute and review the postings as part of their regular activities as well as spontaneously. Think of it as a physical version of a discussion board online. Post a new poster strip each week with the prompt that invites them to share their ideas. The monthly topics are listed below. Four prompts are provided in each month to get you started, but you will develop your own ideas as you go.

- August: Beginnings
- September: Figurative language
- October: Connections—words that signal text structure and connections (segues)
- November: Painting pictures with words
- December: Alike or different
- January: Plotting with seven basic plots
- February: Flights of fantasy

- March: Cause and effect
- April: Caught in the middle
- May: Nonfiction
- June and July: Illusions, allusions, foreshadowing, and mystery

## Inspirational Highlights

Every writer is an avid reader, and many writers have also thought and talked about reading and writing. For every month, you will find quotations to post every week on an easel in the foyer or office about reading, writing, and thinking. When people enter the school, they will see a symbol of your emphasis on reading and writing in the quotations you choose. The quotes are loosely arranged by month so feel free to move them around by what moves you that week. It is also wonderful to quote the readers and writers in your own community. At least once a month you could ask for contributions and choose one to put on the easel, or read aloud in morning announcements. There are four quotations for each month. Here are a few examples:

*The man who doesn't read good books has no advantage over the man who can't read them.* —Mark Twain (1835–1910)

*There are books so alive that you're always afraid that while you weren't reading, the book has gone and changed, has shifted like a river; while you went on living, it went on living too, and like a river moved on and moved away.* —Marina Tsvetaeva (1892–1941)

*One ought, every day at least, to hear a little song, read a good poem, see a fine picture, and if it were possible, to speak a few reasonable words.* —Johann Wolfgang von Goethe (1749–1832)

## Family Nights

To involve parents in creating a culture of literacy in their homes and supporting literacy efforts from school, consider having parent nights once a month. The goal is to have them learn literacy activities they can make part of their home routines. Whether it's reading aloud to each other, listening to family stories, or talking about their favorite things, families can have fun making more room for reading, writing, and thinking in the way they interact.

Plan to have family nights at the same time each month—say the third Thursday. Of course, holidays and other events get in the way sometimes, but the regularity is important to the event becoming a ritual in the school and family—a cornerstone of the culture. You know, or will soon figure out, the format that works best for your families. Some schools get local restaurants to sponsor one night during the year by providing finger food. Keeping them short, an hour or an hour and a half, and fast paced helps people to feel like they can fit it into their schedules and that it is worth their time. You may want to have faculty there to facilitate the activities with families and talk with them about their books and interests. You could buy a book each month to raffle. Her are the topics for each monthly family night.

- August: *Talking about what you read*
- September: *Reading together*
- October: *Reading to each other*
- November: *Interpreting what you read*
- December: *Poetry for dessert*
- January: *Grandparents as storyteller*
- February: *Favorites*
- March: *Improvisation*
- April: *Art in literature*
- May: *Imagination*

## Your Plan Book for Building a Culture of Literacy

Turn now to page 94 to see all these activities arranged in a plan book format. Add your own ideas or rearrange the ones that are there to fit your school. For an electronic copy, visit http://www.techforlearning.org/literacy

# Month-by-Month Listing of Activities

**August:** Getting Ready to Learn
Book of the month: *Oh, the Places You'll Go!*, by Dr. Seuss
In the halls ... *Beginnings*
Share readers' and writers' recommendations
Inspirational highlights
Writing contest: *Goal-setting and the quest*
Family Night: *Talking about what you read*

**September:** Becoming a Learning Community—Rights and Responsibilities
Book of the month: *Stone Soup*, by Marcia Brown
In the halls ... *Figurative language*
Share readers' and writers' recommendations
Inspirational highlights
Writing contest: *A sense of community, descriptive writing*
Family Night: *Reading together*

**October:** Beginning Where You Are
Book of the month: *Walk On! A Guide for Babies of All Ages*, by Marla Frazee
In the halls ... *Connections—words that signal text structure and connections (segues)*
Inspirational highlights
Writing contest: *Journeys, time sequence, autobiographies*
Family night: *Reading to each other*

**November:** Becoming Authors
Book of the month: *Click, Clack, Moo Cows That Type*, by Doreen Cronin
In the halls ... *Painting pictures with words*
Inspirational highlights
Writing contest: *Poetry*
Family night: *Interpreting what you read*

**December:** The Gift of Reading
Book of the month: *Wild About Books*, by Judy Sierra
In the halls ... *Alike or different*
Inspirational highlights
Writing contest: *Book reviews, compare/contrast*
Family night: *Poetry for dessert*

**January:** Celebrating Progress
Book of the month: *The Daddy Mountain*, by Jules Feiffer
In the halls ... *Plotting with seven basic plots*
Inspirational highlights
Writing contest: *Celebrating progress, problem and solution*
Family night: *Grandparents as storyteller*

**February:** Speaking and Listening
Book of the month: *The Frog Princess: A Tlingit Legend from Alaska,* by Eric A. Kimmel and Rosanne Litzinger
In the halls … *Flights of fancy*
Inspirational highlights
Writing contest: *Fantasy*
Family night: *Favorites*

**March:** Reading to Learn, Writing to Understand
Book of the month: *Why Mosquitoes Buzz in People's Ears,* by Verna Aardema
In the halls … *Cause and effect*
Inspirational highlights
Writing contest: *Cause and effect in folktales*
Family night: *Improvisation*

MONTHLY WRITING CONTEST

**April:** Writing to Communicate Feelings and Ideas
Book of the month: *Waiting for Gregory,* by Kimberly Willis Holt
In the halls … *Caught in the middle*
Inspirational highlights
Writing contest: *Short story about feelings*
Family night: *Art in literature*

**May:** Weaving our stories together
Book of the month: *If You Give A Mouse A Cookie,* by Laura Joffe Numeroff
In the halls … *Nonfiction*
Inspirational highlights
Writing contest: *Partnerships, nonfiction*
Family night: *Nonfiction: reading to Learn*

**June and July:** Read On
Book of the month: *Magic Beach,* by Crockett Johnson
In the halls … Illusions, allusions, foreshadowing and mystery
Inspirational highlights
Writing contest: Mystery

# Chapter 2

# August: Getting Ready to Learn

It's the beginning of the year! Students are excited, teachers are ready, and parents are hopeful this will be a good year for their children. This month's theme, "getting ready to learn" is all about starting out right, talking about goals, how we learn, how we interact with each other, and about beginnings. A new academic year is a fresh start for everyone involved with the children as they have new teachers, new friends. and new things to learn. This month, suggested activities described include:

- Book of the month: *Oh, the Places You'll Go!,* by Dr. Seuss
- In the halls … *Beginnings*
- Share readers' and writers' recommendations
- Inspiration from readers and writers
- Writing contest: *Goal-setting and the quest*
- Family Night: *Talking about what you read*

## Book of the Month

In *Oh, the Places You'll Go!,* by Dr. Seuss, we read about how to start your journey, not waiting for something to happen but making it happen.

Congratulations! Today is your day.

You're off to Great Places! You're off and away!

You have brains in your head. You have feet in your shoes.

You can steer yourself any direction you choose.

You're on your own. And you know what you know.

And YOU are the guy who'll decide where to go.

And will you succeed?

Yes! You will, indeed! (98 and 3/4 percent guaranteed)

Student's needs are as varied as the students themselves. Your goal however, is the same for each and every one of them: tap into their desire to learn and set them on a path of life-long learning. *Oh, the Places You'll Go!* brings a sense of adventure and wonder to starting their learning journey of discovery in the coming year and lets them know that whatever comes their way, they'll have choices and they will succeed!

In a faculty meeting before school starts, read the book out loud, give each teacher a copy of the book and 15 minutes to brainstorm by grade level group ways to use it with their students. Have each group share how they will make curriculum connections and the forms students' responses will take. Set a deadline during the month when student responses need to be posted in the halls.

## In the Halls ... Beginnings

Explore beginnings on the posters in the halls. In the first week, make a heading, "Favorite beginnings" and write a few familiar ones such as: Once upon a time; In the beginning; A long time ago and far away.... During the morning announcements, challenge every class to add their favorite beginnings. Collecting beginnings helps students to see how many different ways there are to begin stories.

Week 1: Favorite beginnings list
Week 2: Excerpts from books that begin this way to show what it signals
Week 3: Conversation bubbles explaining what each beginning signals
Week 4: Stories by student authors/classes using the beginnings

In the second week of the month, add a poster asking students to post beginnings with the names of the books and authors. Put up a few beginnings from the first week with two or more books that use that beginning. This heightens students' attention to beginnings in their own reading and writing. They may begin to notice patterns by genre and by author.

In week three, put up another poster with a few of the beginnings, and invite students to share what the beginning means or signals about what is to come. For example, "Once up on a time" can signal a fairy tale, a timeless story or a take-off on a fairy tale. "It all started when …" signals a flash back, perhaps a long story, or recurring problem. Talking about beginnings gives students insight into how they can use them in their own writing and helps them with comprehension in their reading.

## Share Readers' and Writers' Recommendations

Start a bulletin board near the office or inside it for recommendations of books. Ask the person recommending the book to write the name of the book, the author, and what they liked about the book. Suggest some items at the top of the bulletin board,

*If you like mysteries you will love _____.*
*Have you ever wanted to _____, then you will like _____ because _____.*
*This book got and kept my attention by _____.*
*When you meet the character _____, you won't be able to put down _____.*
*There's nothing better than _____ and that's what the book _____ does.*

## Inspirational Highlights

Each week you can post a quotation on an easel in the foyer or on a bulletin board. It's a conversation starter and signals a culture that is interested in learning from others, in thinking about ideas, and in discussing them. You may want to read the quotation as part of the morning announcements on Monday morning to emphasize it, or you may even want to do a sneak preview on Fridays during announcements, or put just the author or the beginning of the quotation up on Fridays. You will figure out what works for you and creates the most interest.

Consider having "local quotes" on other days of the week, or for one week during the month. "Our own Mrs. Vides" always says, "Books are like potato chips, you can't read just one." You can have people summit their own quotes or other people's quotes any time they hear them so you have a collection. Be sure to enter these local quotes in a book you keep on hand in the office or the media center so the students can revisit them.

*The person who doesn't read good books has no advantage over the person who can't read them.* —Mark Twain (1835–1910)

*There is a great deal of difference between an eager person who wants to read a book and the tired person who wants a book to read.* —G. K. Chesterton (1874–1936)

*Play gives children a chance to practice what they are learning....They have to play with what they know to be true in order to find out more, and then they can use what they learn in new forms of play.* —Fred Rogers (U.S. children's TV personality and author; *Mister Rogers Talks with Parents*, 1983, ch. 5)

*There are books so alive that you're always afraid that while you weren't reading, the book has gone and changed, has shifted like a river; while you went on living, it went on living too, and like a river moved on and moved away. No one has stepped twice into the same river. But did anyone ever step twice into the same book?* —Marina Tsvetaeva (1892–1941; Russian poet; reprinted in A *Captive Spirit: Selected Prose*, ed. and trans. by J. Marin King, 1980. Pushkin and Pugachev, 1937)

## Writing Contest: *Goal-Setting and the Quest*

In a culture of literacy, everyone is a reader and a writer. As discussed in chapter 13, "publishing" student's essays, stories, and poetry is very important. A "local authors" corner in the media center, and having copies in the other places, with a "notes to the author" section in the back of the book all contribute to students feeling like their writing is important and has an audience. Prominently display a copy of the winning story during the month following its creation. Have a "meet the author" session after school one day. Even consider making copies for each class so all the students in the school can read or hear the story read aloud. If you publish a school newsletter, the story, or at least reviews of it could be published in that. The more ways you find to treat the writer and his or her writing seriously, the more interest the contest will generate in writing and being read.

The August writing contest is about goal-setting using the plot structure of "the quest." Any approach to the topic is okay, a personal journey, or the story of someone else, set in the past, present, or future, with the quest achieved or tackled without success. A sample flyer is given below. Provide a writing rubric like the one in chapter 13, "What Makes My Writing Worth Reading?" for students to use in writing, and then use it to score the entries.

## Family Night: *Talking About What You Read*

The Family Night this month is *talking about what you read*. This lays the groundwork for families to talk about the books, magazines, and newspapers they are reading. Even work-related manuals, or papers are interesting for children to hear about if the adults explain why they are interested. ANY exposure to adults reading and talking about what they are reading sends the very strong message that reading is a worthwhile activity throughout your life. My nephew has "read" the paper since he was 3 years old because he sat on his dad's lap every morning while his dad read the paper. Now at 12 years old, he really does read the paper. What started out as just being together, then mimicry of this dad, has become a ritual in his life, as well as his dad's life.

In this family night, plan to begin with a read aloud of a short story such as the book of the month, *Oh the Places You'll Go!* by Dr. Seuss about goal-setting. Stop a couple of times to ask families to talk with one another about what this reminds them of in their own lives, whether they feel the same way or different than the author, and what they like about the language in the story. Then have a collection of books on each table for families to choose one to read together and discuss using the same strategies you modeled (such as text-to-life connections, thinking about language, expressing and comparing feelings to situations).

# AUGUST WRITING CONTEST
## Goal-Setting, The Quest

What are your goals for this year? for life? for tomorrow? What goals have you set and met? One of the basic plots writers use is a "quest" that tells the story someone or a group of people trying to achieve a goal. This is your chance to write about your quest, someone you know, or even a character you make up.

You can write about where the quest came from, what it is, how others have achieved it or how you will achieve it. You could even write about a quest you have already achieved. Did you want to learn how to play basketball or read 100 books in a year, or be a better writer? All of these are quests if they come from your heart's desire.

## Rules

You can ask for help from anyone
You can make it as long or as short as
 you want
You are encouraged to add pictures
You are encouraged to be creative
You must have fun!

## Need Help?

### *What is a goal?*

A plan of action, an aim, intent, purpose, or design to achieve something that ends when you reach it.

### *How does a quest become a plot for a story?*

The hero or heroine wants to get something or someone to fill a lack in his/her life or to get something back that was stolen. The quest requires great strength for the hero to face the many challenges in many different locations.

### *What else?*

Have fun with this! Make yourself a superhero, or dream your way into a future of your own choosing.

# FAMILY NIGHT

## Talking About What You Read

August ____ , 20____

Save the date!

Dear Parents, Families, Friends,

Our "Family Read-In" this month is all about talking about what you read. The "kid culture" of television, toys, and movies is no real match for the excitement of an adult talking about what he or she cares about and having a child ask questions and  the two of them share what they are reading. Sometimes parents don't think their children will be interested in what they are reading, but we'll practice some strategies that make this fun and worthwhile for everyone.

Talking about what you are reading is SO important for your kids. You are modeling what good readers do—they talk about what they are reading to make sense of it for themselves, to make connection to the their lives, and to share with other people, and they hear you talk about the same things.

We will suggest some ways for you and your child to talk about what you read. We really want to develop a culture of literacy in our school and community this year. We will be reading and writing to learn, reading to each other, and reading together. Talking about what you read is part of our culture of literacy.

Looking forward to seeing you there!

# Chapter 3

# September: Becoming a Learning Community

In the beginning of the year, the school is coming together as a learning community. It is a time to share skills and interests, establish a tone of decency, and establish the habits of reading and writing every day. Conversations are beginning about strategies, and teachers and students are assessing where they are in learning to read and write. This month, suggested activities described include:

♦ Rights and responsibilities

♦ Book of the month: *Stone Soup,* by Marcia Brown

♦ In the halls ... *Figurative Language*

♦ Share readers' and writers' recommendations

♦ Inspiration from readers and writers

♦ Writing contest: *A sense of community, descriptive writing*

♦ Family Night: *Reading together*

## Rights and Responsibilities

Below are the student rights and responsibilities adapted from the International Reading Association to pose and refer to in morning announcements. You may even want to roll them out one at a time, talking with the faculty about how to help students understand them. Use the tables below to start the discussion about what you believe as a faculty are students' rights and responsibilities.

| Student Rights |
|---|
| ♦ Have access to books that they can read independently so they can read for pleasure and to learn. |
| ♦ Have people to talk to about what they read so they can reflect on its importance for them. |
| ♦ Have a chance to think about what they read so they can integrate it into what they know, feel, and do. |

| Student Responsibilities |
|---|
| ♦ Learn new strategies to improve their reading so they can be more and more successful in reading more and more complex materials. |
| ♦ Write about what they read to make connections to their ideas, other texts, and learn ways of expressing themselves through writing. |
| ♦ Think out loud about what and how they are reading so other students, teachers, and parents can help them to improve. |

You will want to discuss the teacher rights and responsibilities to be sure teachers have the support they need and understand the expectations for them in a culture of literacy. Use the following tables to develop a shared understanding with your faculty about their rights and responsibilities in a culture of literacy.

| Teacher Rights |
|---|
| ♦ Understand how children learn to read and write. |
| ♦ Have the tools and training to help them make specific diagnoses about what children are good and at and what they need. |
| ♦ Have easy access to books and instructional materials at multiple levels. |
| ♦ Have regular professional development and time to share and plan with colleagues. |

| Teacher Responsibilities |
|---|
| ♦ Model good reading and writing. |
| ♦ Use a variety of instructional groupings: Model good reading for children in large groups, teach them specifically what they need in small groups, conference with children individually to track their progress and hear how they are thinking and feeling about their reading and writing. |
| ♦ Schedule time for students to reflect on what and how they are learning. |
| ♦ Collect samples that show student progress over time. |

Administrators also have rights and responsibilities when it comes to developing literacy. Use the following ideas to discuss administrator rights and responsibilities and how they relate to the student and teacher rights and responsibilities.

| Administrator Rights |
| --- |
| ♦ Understand how children learn to read and write. |
| ♦ Expect all faculty and staff to contribute to every child learning to read and write and to using reading and writing to learn, communicate, and have fun. |
| ♦ Expect all families to read with their children every day. |
| ♦ Allocate the resources to buy books for the library, the classrooms, and special events. |
| ♦ Expect all students to learn to the strategies to be successful readers and writers. |

| Administrator Responsibilities |
| --- |
| ♦ Model good reading and writing strategies |
| ♦ Provide in-service for teachers. Lead monthly discussions about literacy topics. Arrange for teachers to have time to talk and plan. Provide diagnostic tools to help teachers make instructional decisions for students. Expect teachers to help each child develop new, more powerful skills and strategies for reading and writing. |
| ♦ Involve parents and community members in actively supporting literacy development with clear expectations, strategies, ideas and encouragement. |
| ♦ Fill the school with books, poems, and posters about reading and writing. Make the library the hub of the school. |
| ♦ Emphasize literacy with whole-school activities. For example, have "stop everything and read times," and lead whole-school book read-ins. |

## Book of the Month

The book of the month is a story of how strangers become part of a community. In *Stone Soup* by Marcia Brown, three tired and hungry soldiers come upon a town that does not wish to share any of their food with the strangers. They are turned away house after house. One soldier then announces to the town that since all of the town-folk are also starving, "we'll have to make stone soup." Little by little, they suggest things that might make the water and stones taste better. First, salt and pepper for seasoning. Then, "But oh, if there were carrots, it would be much better."

The villagers continue to bring one item after the other to the pot to make the soup better and better. "Great tables were placed in the square. And all around were lighted torches." The soldiers and peasants ate a feast "truly fit for a king" while they danced and sang the night away. In the morning, the soldiers are greeted by the entire village that thank them for, "we shall never go hungry, now that we know how to make soup from stones."

What a wonderful story about the power evoked when a community comes together to work toward a common goal. Spend some time in a faculty meeting talking about how to invite reader response to the book at each grade level. For example:

> First grade: Bring in some stones and a big bucket to make the soup. Have children add the objects in the story or pictures, or words that represent them. After reading the story aloud, and making it available for children to read or listen to, revisit the story with the class as the "soup" that everyone contributes to. Have children put their name cards in the "soup" and say what they want to give to the community of learners. Gifts might be a smile, a laugh, a helping hand, a good listener, a kind word, or patience. All make a great community soup when we all work together.

> Fifth grade: After reading the story aloud, brainstorm similar situations where people do not share. Make a list, then let students work in groups to create stories about these situations in which an event such as the strangers' stone soup changes how people feel about the situation and each other. Offer to have them act out their stories for other classes, as well as post their stories in the hall.

## In the Halls ... Figurative Language

Figurative language brings alive the feelings of being part of a community, describes what the community does, and what it believes. More than the literal place or events, the subtleties of being part of a community, figures of speech say more than what the words mean. The poetics of Robert Frost (http://www.frostfriends.org/figurative.html) is a wonderful reference for different figures of speech with examples from Frost's poems. For example, Frost uses "the road not taken" as a symbol for the choices we don't make. Frost said, *"Every poem I write is figurative in two senses. It will have figures in it, of course; but it's also a figure in itself—a figure for something, and it's made so that you can get more than one figure out of it"* (Robert Frost: A Living Voice by Reginald Cook, p. 235). Week by week you can help students to understand and have fun with figurative language in poetry and prose. In the first week, hang a poster on the wall with different figures of speech and invite students to add to them, graffiti style.

- Week 1: Favorite figures of speech
- Week 2: Excerpts from books with figurative language
- Week 3: Conversation bubbles describing what various figures of speech add to the meaning of the words
- Week 4: Stories/poems/essays by student authors/classes using figures of speech

In the second week, hang another poster with excerpts from books, citing their sources. In the third week, choose some of the most interesting or fun figures of speech and start a third poster. Draw some conversation bubbles to be filled in by students about what the figure of speech connotes. In the fourth week of the month, hang a poster with writings by students with the figures of speech highlighted.

For these weekly activities, you may want to have classes take turns contributing to the posters so there is room for all the ideas and every class doesn't have to contribute every week. Try to have all the grades represented to highlight the developmental continuum.

## Share Readers' and Writers' Recommendations

Have a new set of recommendations on the bulletin board in the office every month. Put last month's reviews in a notebook near the bulletin board. Talk with the faculty about how to solicit reviews. Do they want to have a few students make recommendations each month from their class? Would an upper grade class want to interview the other classes about their favorite books and post them? Does the librarian want to make it part of library visits and activities to solicit reviews? Establish a ritual that defines who will contribute, review, and post the book reviews and when they will do it each month. You may want to do it yourself as a nice way to talk with students on an individual or class basis. Visit a class and get them talking about their favorite books, then ask them to write short reviews on the spot. Older students can recommend their favorites from when they were younger as well as their current favorites. The key is to capture the enthusiasm of the reader!

## Inspirational Highlights

Post one of these each week, or substitute local quotes from teachers, students, and families. Archive the previous month's quotes in a book available in the office or library or both. If you have a Web site, post the collection there too. Think about ways to get people to think about the quotations and discuss them with each other.

*One ought, every day at least, to hear a little song, read a good poem, see a fine picture, and if it were possible, to speak a few reasonable words.* —Johann Wolfgang von Goethe (1749–1832; German dramatist, novelist, poet, and scientist)

*Reading furnishes the mind only with materials of knowledge; it is thinking that makes what we read ours.* —John Locke (1632–1704; British philosopher; *An Essay Concerning Human Understanding*, bk. 4, ch. 3, sect. 23, p. 553, ed. P. Nidditch, Oxford, Clarendon Press, 1975)

*Learning and teaching should not stand on opposite banks and just watch the river flow by; instead, they should embark together on a journey down the water. Through an active, reciprocal exchange, teaching can strengthen learning how to learn.* —Loris Malaguzzi (1920–1994; Italian early childhood education specialist, quoted in *The Hundred Languages of Children*, ch. 3, by Carolyn Edwards, 1993)

*Language is the soul of intellect, and reading is the essential process by which that intellect is cultivated beyond the commonplace experiences of everyday life.* —Charles Scribner Jr. (*Publishers Weekly*, March 30, 1984)

## Writing Contest: *A Sense of Community, Descriptive Writing*

This month's contest invites students to write about the school's culture of literacy. What is their vision? What will help them to be a strong reader and writer? As they say, "Out of the mouths of babes" comes wisdom sometimes, so you can look forward to some interesting ideas that you may be able to incorporate into your literacy plan book.

If you want to provide scaffolding, provide students with a sample organizer to write down their ideas. Encourage them to use lots of adjectives in the clouds.

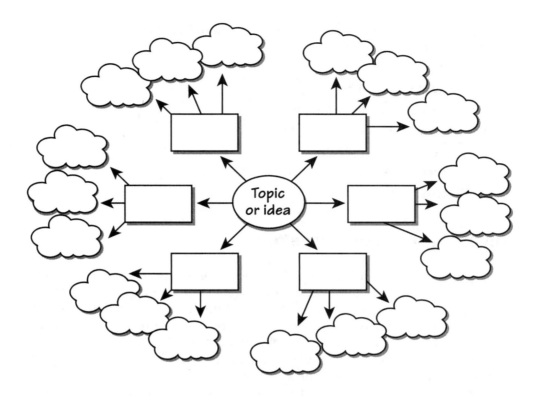

Then encourage them to explore synonyms, antonyms, and figurative language to improve the descriptions of their ideal school.

| Adjectives | Synonyms | Antonyms | Figures of Speech |
|---|---|---|---|
| Playful | Full of fun<br>Mischievous<br>High-spirited<br>Teasing | Subdued<br>Serious<br>Stiff<br>Sober | Students would toy with ideas like cats with yarn, pushing and pulling on them, never running out of ways to bat around that ball of yarn until it unravels for them. |
|  |  |  |  |
|  |  |  |  |
|  |  |  |  |
|  |  |  |  |

Then provide a writing process if your district or state has one, or use a standard process such as this one:

- Prewriting to collect ideas;
- Organize and elaborate on ideas;
- Choose a focus and write it clearly;
- Develop a rough draft;
- Get feedback and reflect on your draft to revise it; and
- Rewrite and publish.

## Family Night: *Reading Together*

The goal of this family night is to have families experience a lot of different ways they can read together. If you have a very active group, set it up so they move from table to table to try each method. If you have a more reserved group that might feel self-conscious about moving all the time, or be distracted by it, have cards on each table for them to choose from to try each method. Be sure to provide lots of great books on the tables so each family can read several books as they try the strategies.

For the family "Family Read-In," have reading materials and different ways of reading together at each table.

- Read every other line
- Read every other page
- Read together at the same time—choral reading
- One person "reads" the pictures, the other reads the words aloud
- One person reads aloud and the other one thinks about it and retells it
- One person reads the whole piece, then the other reads it
- Read dialog in roles
- One person reads, the other acts out what is happening
- The two people take turns reading and predicting what will happen next
- Take turns reading and drawing what is happening

# SEPTEMBER WRITING CONTEST

## A Sense of Community: A Descriptive Essay

### Culture of Literacy—A School Vision

A community of literacy means that all students, teachers, and parents are committed to helping each other become better readers and writers through practice and hard fun. Getting everyone involved is the best way to make this happen.

What is your vision of how our school should be to help every single boy and girl to learn to read and write well and to be able to learn through reading? This is your chance to imagine anything you think might work. What will you and your friends be reading, writing, learning? How will you be learning? What will be different from now? Who will help? Will you be reading and writing to people all over the world? Will you be a famous author of children's books? Will you read books with a magical lens that draws pictures of everything you read? Remember to show the readers your vision with lots of adjectives rather just than telling them.

## Rules

You can make it as long or as short as you want
You are encouraged to add pictures
You are encouraged to be creative
You must have fun!

## Need Help?

### What is literacy?

The ability to read, write, listen, and speak

### What is your community?

All those you spend time with and where you spend your time. Think about what makes you feel part of your community to design your ideal community of readers and writers.

### What else can you do?

Start a community, such as a reading club, a writer's circle, or a special interest group.

# FAMILY NIGHT

## Reading Together

September ___ , 20____
Save the date!

Dear Parents, Families, Friends,

Our "Family Read-In" this month is all about *Reading Together.* You will have the opportunity to read dialog in roles, have one person read while the other acts out the story, read books where you challenge each other to figure out what is going to happen next in the story, read and draw the story, and much more.

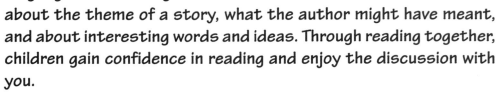

Reading together benefits children's language and thinking skills. You can talk about the theme of a story, what the author might have meant, and about interesting words and ideas. Through reading together, children gain confidence in reading and enjoy the discussion with you.

Join us in this night of reading together and help your child see reading as a pleasurable activity where they can learn and connect with you and others in the family. We will have lots of fun books for you to choose from and ideas for things to talk about as you read together with your child.

Looking forward to seeing you there!

# Chapter 4

# October:
# Beginning Where You Are

The new beginning that each school represents is wonderful for each child has a fresh start. To hold on to that feeling of potential that comes with beginnings, focus on learning as a process that always begins where *you* are. Sometimes learning seems like an all or nothing game, a right or wrong test, or even worse, a timed test that you only do once. In a culture devoted to literacy, students feel they can begin where they are and that they will be supported in the fits and starts that happen in real learning. Their teachers and families stress that sometimes you learn something fast and other times, it takes a long time to learn something. They know that every child comes to each learning experience with different backgrounds, experience, skills, and preconceptions that shape their learning. The goal in October is to get everyone talking about these things so they are explicitly supported in the culture. This month, suggested activities described include:

- ♦ Book of the month: *Walk On! A Guide for Babies of All Ages*, by Marla Frazee
- ♦ In the halls … Connections—words that signal text structure and connections (segues)
- ♦ Inspiration from readers and writers
- ♦ Writing contest: *Journeys, time sequence, autobiography*
- ♦ Family night: *Reading to each other*

## Book of the Month

In ***Walk On! A Guide for Babies of All Ages***, by Marla Frazee we remember what is was like to learn the basics.

Is sitting there on your bottom getting boring?

Has lying around all the time become entirely unacceptable?

It is time to learn how to walk!

Stand on your own two feet.

Then look for some support. But choose wisely for "what you think will support you won't"

Now. Get a grip. Pull yourself up. Stand. You are now ready for walking.

Important! Don't look down at your feet. Look toward where you are going. Imagine yourself as already there.

The many challenges of a young child learning to walk are the very same that we all must face each day as we start down a new road, head off on a great adventure, or experience our first day of school. Marla Frazee writes about the challenges and obstacles for those first steps to remind us to "see how different everything looks from here," find "support," "let go," "make sure the path ahead of you is clear," and before long, "baby, you are walking!"

By October, students should be comfortable choosing reading books at a "just right" level. They are learning new strategies for making sense of words, and sentences and stories. They are learning to write paragraphs and think about stories. They are in "learning mode" and ready for the kind of feedback that comes naturally in a learning environment, just like the baby learning to walk.

## In the Halls … Segues—Words That Signal Text Structure and Connections

Segue (pronounced segway) comes from the Latin word *seguire*, "to follow." They are those wonderful words and phrases that draw the reader along, connecting ideas without interruption, easing transitions, and making connections. A good segue makes a shift to a new topic feel like a natural extension of the conversation. From little words, like "then" to phrases such as, "holding his breath" to time sequence words such as "first, second, third" segues create a flow of ideas. Use a pattern for the hall posters from the earlier months. In the first week, ask for examples, followed by examples from specific books in the second week. In the third week, look at connotations of the segues and in the fourth week, ask for examples from student authors. Collect the segues and archive them in the writing resource center in a book or make a poster that can be duplicated for classrooms so students have a ready reference for smooth transitions.

- Week 1: Favorite segues
- Week 2: Excerpts from books with great segues
- Week 3: Conversation bubbles describing what various segues mean
- Week 4: Stories/poems/essays by student authors/classes using segues

## Share Readers' and Writers' Recommendations

Check in with teachers on how the rituals established last month are working to solicit book reviews. Are you getting at least three to four recommendations per week? Are students paying attention to them? Do you hear students talking about the recommendations? Is there a waiting list for the books in the library? Revise the plan if needed. Celebrate the successes and discuss the effects of having student and teacher recommendations a regular part of the school week.

## Inspirational Highlights

This month's inspirational quotes are about the effect of reading on our lives and thoughts. Consider discussing one or more of these with faculty in a meeting to get them thinking about how they might use them for discussion and elicit some "local quotes" from students about the effect of reading on them. Prompts might include:

- Reading makes me …
- If I never read again …
- A day without reading is like a day without …
- Without reading, life would be …
- I never would have … if I hadn't read …

*Reading made Don Quixote a gentleman. Believing what he read made him mad.* —George Bernard Shaw (1856–1950; Irish dramatist and socialist)

*People say that life is the thing, but I prefer reading.* —Logan Pearsall Smith (1865–1946; U.S. essayist, aphorist; Afterthoughts, "Myself," 1931)

*It would be worth the while to select our reading, for books are the society we keep; to read only the serenely true; never statistics, nor fiction, nor news, nor reports, nor periodicals, but only great poems, and when they failed, read them again, or perchance write more. Instead of other sacrifice, we might offer up our perfect (teleia) thoughts to the gods daily, in hymns or psalms. For we should be at the helm at least once a day.* —Henry David Thoreau (1817–1862; U.S. philosopher, author, and naturalist, "A Week on the Concord and Merrimack Rivers," 1849, in *The Writings of Henry David Thoreau*, vol. 1, p. 98, Houghton Mifflin, 1906)

*Never read a book through merely because you have begun it.* —John Witherspoon (1723–1794; U.S. clergyman, educator, and politician)

## Writing Contest: *Journeys, Time Sequence, Autobiography*

This month's writing contest is about journeys and telling them in time and space. The stories can be real or imagined, go backwards or forwards, begin in the middle, and have no end. The only rule is that they be autobiographical so students have a chance to experiment with that genre. Encourage students to use different forms of the autobiography such as letters, diaries and journals.

Create a display of autobiographies in the office and library. Put all the autobiographies in the classroom libraries in a genre basket or on a shelf together so students can browse through them for ideas.

## Family Night: *Reading to Each Other*

For this month's family night, have lots of fun short pieces for families to read. At each table have poems, short stories, limericks, and jokes of different reading levels. Families take turns reading at the table, like they would at meals, in the car, and at family gatherings. Have things to read, rap, and sing. Give each family a packet to get them started, and recommend books, magazines, and student newspapers to read from. For more suggestions, see chapter 19.

# OCTOBER WRITING CONTEST

## Journeys, Time Sequence, and Autobiographies

### Beginning Where You Are—Your Journey

During your life you will have many journeys. Some will take you to new places and some will take you to new ideas and many will do both. Many writers have told wonderful stories about their journeys like *Golden Bear* by Ruth Young about a little boy and bear that learn to play the violin, talk to a ladybug, make mudpies, wish on stars, and dream together.

Tell a story about where your journey began and where it is going. What have you done? What have you learned? What has meant the most to you and where you would like to go and do in the future? What have you dreamt?

### Rules

You can make it as long or as short as you want
You are encouraged to add pictures
You are encouraged to be creative
You must have fun!

## Need Help?

### *What is your journey?*

Everywhere you are thinking of going and everywhere you have been.

### *What is an autobiography?*

The story of your life told by you. This genre started in the fifteenth century.

It can be letters, diaries, journals, memoirs, or reminiscences.

### *What is a time sequence?*

A way in which things follow after each other in space or time.

# FAMILY NIGHT

## Reading to Each Other

*October ___ , 20____*
*Save the date!*

Dear Parents, Families, Friends,

Our "Family Read In" this month is all about *reading to each other.* There are many times during the day that families can boost literacy skills in their children and reading to each other is one of them. Reading to each other allows for a quite time where you can reconnect, share ideas, demonstrate learning. Whether your child can already read or is just beginning to read, the more they hear and enjoy language, the more fluent they will become.

When your hands are busy with cooking or cleaning up, ask your child to read to you. If they have difficulty, ask them to read it again, and think about what makes sense. Talk through what might work in the context of the sentence and paragraph. If there is a new word, you can talk about what it means, its roots or parts, and other words that are alike or different. Ask your child to stop after each page or at natural breaks and talk to you about what is happening and what it reminds them of.

This month, we have lots of short pieces for you and your family to read. At each table you might find poems, short stories, songs, fairy tales, and age appropriate books that have importance and meaning for any age. You are also invited to bring your favorite pieces to read to each other.

Looking forward to seeing you all there!

# Chapter 5

# November: Becoming Authors

This month's theme is to explore what it means to be an author, how satisfying it can be to put words to paper and at the same time how challenging it can be, how powerful words can be in communicating, and how words can paint pictures. The book of the month is about how the barnyard animals use the power of writing to create change. You will notice that the writing contest this month is on poetry to come before the holiday rush. Student poems created this month can be displayed and read during December's Family Night, Poetry for Dessert. This month, suggested activities include:

- Book of the month: *Click, Clack, Moo Cows That Type,* by Doreen Cronin
- In the halls … Painting pictures with words
- Inspiration from readers and writers
- Writing contest: *Poetry*
- Family night: *Interpreting what you read*

## Book of the Month

In *Click, Clack, Moo Cows That Type*, by Doreen Cronin, "Farmer Brown has a problem. His cows like to type. All day long he hears click, clack, moo. Click, clack, moo. Clickety, clack, moo." The cows write to Farmer Brown asking for simple items to make their lives a little better. First, because "the barn is very cold at night," they ask for electric blankets. He refuses. The cows write again saying, "Sorry. We're closed. No milk today." The chickens are also cold at night and make a similar request. Again, Farmer Brown refuses. The cow's new note reads, "Closed. No milk. No eggs." Again Farmer Brown demands milk and eggs. After holding an emergency meeting, the cows again write to Farmer Brown saying, "We will exchange our typewriter for electric blankets." Farmer Brown agrees and the cows and chickens have prevailed. The twist comes with the ducks.

The power of words, ideas, and knowledge are all made clear in this very simple work. Doreen Cronin takes these difficult ideas and brings them to children. The cows are authors and work together to get what they feel is fair. It is clear that by the end of the book that the ideas of the cows and chickens are spreading throughout the farm. By November students are writing with a purpose and thinking about their audiences.

## In the Halls ... Painting Pictures With Words

Poems do not have a corner on painting pictures with words, but they certainly focus on it. Imagery uses the five senses to create the impression of being there, seeing with your own eyes, hearing the sounds of another time or place, or smelling the goodness of a home cooked meal, or the foulness of rotten garbage. When children discover imagery, their writing improves by leaps and bounds, and they simply have more fun with it. In the halls this month, continue the pattern of collecting ideas, identifying examples from literature, making conversation bubbles about connotations and then posting student writing.

- ◆ Week 1: Favorite imagery (from Robert Frost: The roar of trees, the crystal shells of ice, smelling green, the clouds were low and hairy, blueberries as big as your thumb; from Shel Silverstein's "Sarah Cynthia Sylvia Stout": crusts of black burned buttered toast, gloppy glumps of cold outmeal, rubbery, blubbery macaroni, cold French fries and rancid meat)

- ◆ Week 2: Excerpts from poems with imagery, like the following:

> A piece of the sky
> Broke off and fell
> Through the crack in the ceiling
> Right into my soup
> > Shel Silverstein, *Sky Seasoning*

> The first cold shower
> Even the monkey seems to want
> a little coat of straw
> > Basho haiku classic

> Wearing her
> "World's Best Mom" T-shirt,
> She wallops the whining kid.
> > — Flossie Pflug from *Senryu Magazine*, vol. 25

> Twas brillig, and the slithy toves
> Did gyre and gimble in the wabe
> All mimsy were the borogoves
> And the mome raths outgrabe
> —Lewis Carroll, *Jabberwocky*

- ◆ Week 3: Conversation bubbles describing what imagery brings to mind
- ◆ Week 4: Poems by student authors/classes using vivid imagery

## Share Readers' and Writers' Recommendations

Ask teachers and students to share their recommendations live in the morning announcements, or at the beginning of the lunch period, or even at Family Nights. Budget for multiple copies of the most popular titles. Be sure to archive the recommendations in the library and/or on the Web site for future browsing. Check in with the faculty to see if students are starting to spontaneously recommend books to each other, resulting in groups of students who share a reading history and preferences.

## Inspirational Highlights

This month's inspirational quotes are about the inevitable interplay between reader and text as the words provoke feelings, memories and experiences. Ask teachers and students for their own quotes about how books engage them. Some prompts could include:

- ◆ Reading makes me ….
- ◆ When I read something that makes me see it in my mind's eye …
- ◆ Reading is like dreaming because ….
- ◆ When I read, time …
- ◆ Reading reminds me that ….

*Reading a book is like rewriting it for yourself.… You bring to a novel, anything you read, all your experience of the world. You bring your history and you read it in your own terms.* —Angela Carter (1940–1992; British author; *Marxism Today*, London, January 1985)

*Writing and reading is to me synonymous with existing.* —Gertrude Stein (1874-1946; U.S. author and patron of the arts)

*Like dreaming, reading performs the prodigious task of carrying us off to other worlds. But reading is not dreaming because books, unlike dreams, are subject to our will: they envelop us in alternative realities only because we give them explicit permission to do so. Books are the dreams we would most like to have, and, like dreams, they have the power to change consciousness, turning sadness to laughter and anxious introspection to the relaxed contemplation of some other time and place.* —Victor Null (South African educator and psychologist; *Lost in a Book: The Psychology of Reading for Pleasure*, Introduction, Yale University Press, 1988)

*Don't join the book burners. Don't think you're going to conceal faults by concealing evidence that they ever existed. Don't be afraid to go in your library and read every book.* —Dwight D. Eisenhower (1890–1969; 34th president of the United States, 1953-1961)

## Writing Contest: *Poetry*

One reason people wrote poetry was to remember stories and retell them. The structure, rhyme, and imagery helped with remembering the stories. The oldest poem we know about is the *Epic of Gilgamesh* from Sumer in Mesopotamia/Iraq. Other familiar poems are the *Iliad* and the *Odyssey*, Chaucer's *Canterbury Tales*. The Polish historian of aesthetics, Wladyslaw Tatarkiewicz, in a paper on "The Concept of Poetry," traces the evolution to two concepts of poetry: poetry an art based on language, and poetry to express a state of mind.

For the writing contest, encourage students to use poetic forms to play with language and to capture humorous, everyday or unusual situations.

## Family Night: *Interpreting What You Read*

At a faculty meeting, or through a notice, ask each teacher to submit a short story and a poem with multiple choice literal questions and interpretive questions for each (at least five questions/text) to use for this family night. Sample questions could be:

◆ What would you say this story is about, in your own words?

◆ What really got your attention? (the main idea, how it was written, characters, information?)

- What do you think the author was trying to do or say?
- What else have you read that comes to mind when you read this?
- What connections can you make between this and your own life?

Use a "think, pair, share" type approach to the activity by having families talk together, then share with others at the table to come up with their best answers. Then share with the whole group. If you find quieter activities work better with your families, number the question cards and answers so they can record them on a card, then come up with an answer key to check them. Have prizes be copies of the books or poems, or bookmarks designed by students. ◆

# NOVEMBER WRITING CONTEST

## Poetry

It is important to have your ideas heard by others and to be able to write in a way that captures their interest and attention. You might find that poetry is a way you can express yourself. Did you know we have an official poet for the country called a poet laureate? You could be the next laureate!

Write and perhaps illustrate a poem. Use your imagination and creativity to give feeling and emotion to your poem.

## Rules

You can make it as long or as short as you want
You are encouraged to add pictures
You are encouraged to be creative
You must have fun!

## Need Help?

### What is poetry?

Poetry is a type of writing where the sound and meaning of words are combined to create ideas and feelings.

### Where to read some wonderful poems ...

There are many Internet sites that contain many poems. Read works by Shel Silverstein who wrote about everyday kid situations or Patricia Hubbell whose poems are filled with rhymes and song.

### What else?

Read aloud poetry to feel how it sounds in your mouth. Have fun using words that have similar beginning sounds like the sweet smell of success or a dime a dozen.

# FAMILY NIGHT

## Interpreting What You Read

*November ____ , 20____*
*Save the date!*

Dear Parents, Families, Friends,

Our "Family Read-In" this month is *"Quiz Show Night!"* This family literature activity focuses on interpreting what we read. You and your child(ren) will read a short story, poem, or newspaper article at each table and then answer questions about it. You will put your heads together to come up with one answer as a family team.

Some of the questions will be literal—you can point to the answer in the text. Other questions will be interpretive—you will need to read between the lines for the answer.

Interpreting is a powerful skill that adults use all the time to make sense of what they read. Writers depend on readers being able to read between the lines to completely understand what they mean. We'll have fun with both literal and interpretive questions on Family Night this month.

Looking forward to seeing you all there!

# Chapter 6

# December: The Gift of Reading

It's a good time to celebrate the gift of reading. It's a great time to give and use recommendations, comparing and contrasting books to choose ones for presents. This month, the halls will be filled with comparisons. The poetry from last month will be a special present for parents. This month's activities include:

- Book of the month: *Wild About Books,* by Judy Sierra
- In the halls ... Alike or different
- Inspiration from readers and writers
- Writing contest: *Book reviews, compare/contrast*
- Family night: *Poetry for dessert*

## Book of the Month

In *Wild About Books,* by Judy Sierra, "When the Springfield librarian, Molly McGrew, by mistake drove her bookmobile into the zoo," at first the animals were shy but quickly learned what to do. "In a flash, every beast in the zoo was stampeding to learn about this new something called reading ... Tasmanian devils found books so exciting that soon they had given up fighting for writing." The excitement for reading grows and grows until the animals create and run their very own library. So remember, "When you visit the zoo now, you surely won't mind if the animals seem just a bit hard to find—they are snug in the niches, their nests, and their nooks, going wild, simply wild about wonderful books."

This book by Judy Sierra and Marc Brown is dedicated to Theodore Seuss Geisel. It is a beautifully illustrated tale where even the animals of the zoo come to love reading and books. The animals create their own works, read them aloud to others, and strengthen their knowledge and interests. And like the gazelle that "couldn't spell very well, like everyone else, she had stories to tell." December is time to bring out the storytellers in your school, and have them give the gift of their own stories or books by others as presents during the holidays.

## In the Halls... Alike Or Different

Have fun on the hall posters with similarities and differences. In week 1 put a word or phrase in the center of a split concept map with room for similarities on one side and differences on the other side. For example, the sunrise could be described as a ball of fire rising from the horizon, or different than the quiet fading of the light at night.

- ◆ Week 1: Similarities and differences
- ◆ Week 2: Excerpts from books with comparisons
- ◆ Week 3: Conversation bubbles to describe situations, people, places and things through compare/contrast
- ◆ Week 4: Stories/poems/essays by student authors/classes using compare/contrast

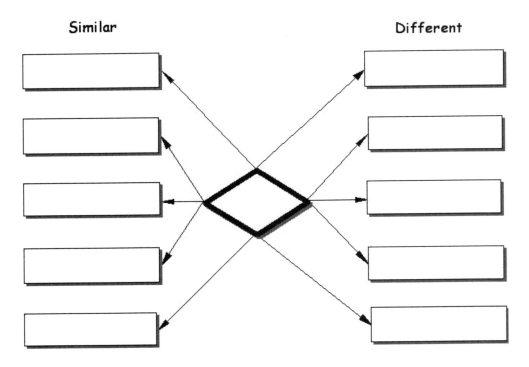

## Share Readers' and Writers' Recommendations

Keep up the bulletin board and announcements about recommended books. Consider having a book fair or local bookseller come in for family night so families can buy books for gifts.

## Inspirational Highlights

Use this month's quotes to talk about gratitude. People are grateful for being able to read, for reading well, for finding time to read often, for having lots of books to read, and for begin able to read the writing of friends. To get students started on their "local quotes" consider the following prompts:

- ◆ I am grateful for being able to read …
- ◆ I will always be grateful for reading …
- ◆ I am grateful I can read because …
- ◆ I appreciate having time to read …

*When I read a book I seem to read it with my eyes only, but now and then I come across a passage, perhaps only a phrase, which has a meaning for me, and it becomes part of me.* —W. Somerset Maugham (1874–1965; *Of Human Bondage*, 1915)

*If you can read this, thank a teacher.* —Anonymous teacher

*In a real sense, people who have read good literature have lived more than people who cannot or will not read. It is not true that we have only one life to live; if we can read, we can live as many more lives and as many kinds of lives as we wish.* —S.I. Hayakawa (1906–1992; Canadian-born U.S. educator, semanticist, and senator; *Language in Thought and Action*, ch. 2, Harcourt Brace, 1939)

*Properly, we should read for power. A person reading should be a person intensely alive. The book should be a ball of light in one's hand.* Ezra Pound (1885– 1972, U.S. poet)

## Writing Contest: *Book Reviews, Compare/Contrast*

A good book review tells you enough to make up your own mind while at the same time hearing how someone else reacted. Of course, the book reviewer hopes to persuade you that his or her opinion of the book so you will either read or not read the book. But a good reviewer gives you enough insight into the book to be able to disagree. Part of how book reviews are crafted is to compare and contrast the book with other texts in the same genre, field, or by the same author. Putting the book into context this ways helps establish the expectations for what the book "should" be and how it stands up against these expectations. If the book recommendations have been going strong through the morning announcements, in the library displays, and in the classroom, students should be prepared to write reviews of their own. You may wish to allow submissions by groups, particularly in younger students, facilitated by the teacher.

## Family Night: *Poetry for Dessert*

Invite children to read the poems they wrote last month, beginning with the writing contest winners for each grade level. Then choose a variety of ages and subjects for other poems to be read aloud. Invite parents to bring their own or favorite poetry to read. Make copies of the poems for the poets to give out at their tables. Start the evening off with a couple of poems for the whole group, then position the poets at a table in shifts so they are reading for 5-10 minutes, then joining the listeners. Have response cards on the table that listeners can use to react to each poem. For example:

- This poem reminds me of …
- I love the language in the part …
- This poem created a picture in my mind of …
- I like how you …
- The language you used to describe … was …

# DECEMBER WRITING CONTEST

## Book Review:
## Compare and Contrast

You've seen, heard and read reviews of books this year by teachers and other students. Now is your chance to write a book review using compare and contrast. Choose a book to review and in your review, write about how it is like or different from at least three other books.

This is the time of year many people give and receive books for presents. Your review may influence people to buy the books you talk about.

## Rules

You can make it as long or as short as
   you want
You are encouraged to add pictures
You are encouraged to be creative
You must have fun!

# Need Help?

### *What is a book review?*

A book review should let the reader know what the book is about, what the reviewer likes and dislikes about the book and why, and some background about the author and other writing that helps the reader to form an opinion of the book.

### *How to compare and contrast ...*

Choose some characteristics of the books to compare and contrast. Describe how they are alike or different in important ways.

### *What else?*

Be sure to tell enough about the book so people have their own information about the plot, the setting, the characters and the problem in the book. Add your own opinions about how good the book is and who might like it. You can compare it to other books by the same author, in the same genre, or on the same topic.

# FAMILY NIGHT

## Poetry for Desert

*December ___ , 20____*
*Save the date!*

Dear Parents, Families, Friends,

Our "Family Read-In" this month is *Poetry for Dessert*. Enjoy an evening of rhymes and limericks, sonnets and haiku, epics and ballads, cinquains and acrostics ... just to name a few. Students have written their own poems and will recite them for you. You are also invited to recite a poem of your own like Brad did here.

Down the slide
On to the next
Moving as fast as possible
For another go around

On the merry-go-round
Head just off the ground
Spinning world closer to reality
Blood as rich as the sea of voices
The ride might be over
But the familiar feeling never ends

Up the ladder again
To the very top
Perched where the view is vast
The wiser child makes it last

Poetry celebrates language and is as luscious as dessert when it is read out loud. You may start a tradition at your house to have poetry for dessert.
Looking forward to seeing you all there! Bring your favorite poem to share.

# Chapter 7

# January: Celebrating Progress

January is a good time to check in on and celebrate progress. Assessing progress in the first half of the year can make a big difference in how much progress is made in the second half of the year. This month, the book *The Daddy Mountain,* is about doing something you know is hard. Knowing the seven basic plots makes something that could be hard—understanding so many different stories—easy. In the writing contest, students write about progress using the problem and solution nonfiction structure. At the Family Night, grandparents and other adults are asked to come and share their stories of progress of triumph.

- Book of the month: *The Daddy Mountain,* by Jules Feiffer
- In the halls … Plotting with seven basic plots
- Inspiration from readers and writers
- Writing contest: *Celebrating progress, problem, and solution*
- Family night: *Grandparents as storyteller*

## Book of the Month

In *The Daddy Mountain,* by Jules Feiffer, a little girl makes progress through great effort.

"Watch me," says the little red-headed girl, "I'm getting ready to climb the Daddy Mountain." After a quick drink she's off. "I have to be brave," she describes. "You have to be careful … you have to be brave … I hold on tight and go not too fast. It's harder than you think…. Inches from the top! I can't believe that I am so brave … I climbed the Daddy Mountain," she proclaims.

With midyear assessments, there is an opportunity to celebrate progress. Jules Feiffer's book illustrates progress and triumph. The little red-haired girl is brave, is careful, holds on tight, does not go too fast, and is *so* brave. She persists and in the end we can all celebrate her progress. Find ways to celebrate everyone's personal records. Like any individual sport, it is the personal records that matter the most.

## In the Halls ... Plotting With Seven Basic Plots

Post the seven basic plots on the first week's hall poster. They are described in more detail in chapter 15. Just list the titles, and have more description for the teachers. You can add "sad" or "bad guys" to tragedy, "funny" to comedy, "another chance" to rebirth, and "hero" to the quest to make the plots understandable to younger children.

- Overcoming the monster: A tale of conflict typically recounts the hero's ordeals, an escape from death, and ends with a community or the world itself saved from evil.

- Rags to riches: *Cinderella*, *The Ugly Duckling*, *David Copperfield*, and other stories that tell of modest, downtrodden characters whose special talents or beauty are finally revealed to the world for a happy ending.

- The quest (hero): Features a hero, normally joined by sidekicks, traveling the world, and fighting to overcome evil and secure a priceless treasure.

- Voyage and return: From *Alice in Wonderland* to Goldilocks to *The Time Machine*, the characters either choose a voyage or fall into a strange world that they must figure out how to return from. Children love the story of Hansel and Gretel's clever idea of bread crumbs and try it out on their own mini-adventures.

- Comedy (funny): Confusion reigns until at last the hero and heroine act out of character by making mistakes and laughing are united in love or things work out for the star of the show.

- Tragedy (sad, bad guys): Portrays human overreaching and its terrible consequences. The bad guys always lose in children's stories and movies. They are bigger than life, supremely overconfident and inevitably fail.

- Rebirth (another chance): Centers on characters such as Dickens's *Scrooge* and *Snow White*, telling the story of their transformations.

Week 1: Post the seven plots so children can describe stories or characters for each

Week 2: Post the seven plots again, so children can list the names of stories, books, or poems for each one

Week 3: Conversation bubbles around each plot describe what always happens in that plot

Week 4: Post stories/poems/essays by student authors/classes categorized by the seven plots

## Share Readers' and Writers' Recommendations

Continue highlighting student and teacher recommendations for books. By now you have figured out what solicits recommendations and gets people to pay attention to them. Continue to build toward having students make spontaneous recommendations to each other, share books and write recommendations so they feel the pride that comes with others taking their recommendations.

## Inspirational Highlights

Remember to solicit some "local quotes" and have teachers find a way to use the quote of the week with students in their classes.

*Writing is an exploration. You start from nothing and learn as you go.*
—E. L. (Edgar Lawrence) Doctorow (b. 1931; U.S. novelist; Interview in *Writers at Work*, Eighth Series, ed. George Plimpton, 1988).

*True ease in writing comes from art, not chance,*
*As those move easiest who have learn'd to dance.*
*'Tis not enough no harshness gives offence,*
*The sound must seem an echo to the sense.*
—Alexander Pope (1688–1744; British poet; Essay on Criticism (Fr. II) … Poetical Works [Alexander Pope]. Herbert Davis, ed., 1978, reprinted 1990, Oxford University Press).

*Reading maketh a full man; conference a ready man; and writing an exact man.* —Francis Bacon (1561–1626; British philosopher, essayist, and statesman; Essays, "Of Studies," 1597-1625).

*With one day's reading a man may have the key in his hands.* —Ezra Pound (1885–1972; U.S. poet and critic; Canto 74, Pisan Cantos, 1948). In contrast, Pound had once confided to William Carlos Williams that, *"It is not necessary to read everything in a book in order to speak intelligently of it,"* adding, *"Don't tell everybody I said so."* (Quoted in Williams' Kora in Hell, 1920, p. 13).

## Writing Contest: *Celebrating Progress, Problem and Solution*

This month's writing contest can be serious or playful, as the flyer shows. Grandpa's story is funny, and it shows how problems come up and are solved. Encourage teachers and students to write about problems great and small and how people overcome them and celebrate.

## Family Night: *Grandparents as Storyteller*

The family night activities build on the writing contest idea, inviting family members to tell stories about problems and solutions in their lives. You might start with a story of your own, or read *The Daddy Mountain*. Use a "think, pair, share" strategy to get families telling each other their stories, or encourage children to remember the stories to write about later in class as ways to extend the audience or the stories. If some classes are looking at family histories, encourage children to write up more stories from their families to add to the "family trees" and other activities.

- ◆ Ask a few grandparents to be ready to tell stories at a few tables.
- ◆ Have some students ready to tell some family stories at a table.
- ◆ After this first round, encourage the storyteller to ask the group for another story. "Who has a story like this one? Did this story make you think of a story? Please share it."
- ◆ Have a shell, rock, ball, or other object for the storyteller to hold, and then pass on to the next storyteller.

# JANUARY WRITING CONTEST

## Celebrating Progress,
## Problems, and Solutions

January brings with it a new year and a reminder that the cycle of learning and growing continues. We often look back over the year to see what progress we have made. How have you done so far this year compared to how you would like to be doing? What have you worked very hard at to accomplish and feel particularly proud of?

Create a poster that shows one of your accomplishments from this year or another time in your life. Draw the path you took to be successful. Showing the problems you had and the solutions you came up with to keep moving forward. Include pictures and drawings of yourself, your challenges, and your successes. Then write about what you illustrated in your poster.

## Rules

You can make it as long or as short as you want
You are encouraged to add pictures
You are encouraged to be creative
You must have fun!

## Need Help?

### *What is progress?*

The act of moving forward towards a goal. You often run into problems and have to find solutions to move forward.

### *What is success?*

Accomplishing what you set out to do and knowing how you did it.

### *What is the problem-solution organization for nonfiction?*

A problem comes up and the main character looks for a solution to keep moving forward. The problem is described in detail so it is clear why it is a problem. Sometimes it takes a lot of effort to find a solution that works. In the end, the success of the solution to solve the problem is described.

# FAMILY NIGHT

## Grandparents as Storytellers
### January ___ , 20____
### Save the date!

Dear Parents, Families, Friends,

Our "Family Read-In" this month is about *Grandparents as Storytellers*. Storytelling needs new audiences all the time. Front porches and campfires are often few and far between, so make this Family Night your campfire time. Invite your grandparents and special friends from the community to join us and share with us their favorite stories about setting goals, problems they have faced and solutions they have found. How have they celebrated progress in their lives?

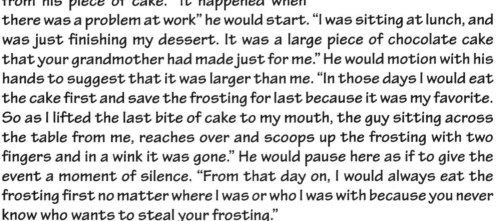

My grandfather's favorite story was about why he always ate the frosting first from his piece of cake. "It happened when there was a problem at work" he would start. "I was sitting at lunch, and was just finishing my dessert. It was a large piece of chocolate cake that your grandmother had made just for me." He would motion with his hands to suggest that it was larger than me. "In those days I would eat the cake first and save the frosting for last because it was my favorite. So as I lifted the last bite of cake to my mouth, the guy sitting across the table from me, reaches over and scoops up the frosting with two fingers and in a wink it was gone." He would pause here as if to give the event a moment of silence. "From that day on, I would always eat the frosting first no matter where I was or who I was with because you never know who wants to steal your frosting."

Looking forward to seeing you there with your storytellers and their stories!

# Chapter 8

# February:
# Speaking and Listening

Speaking and listening develop and thrive in a natural laboratory for language development. Children want to be heard and to interact with those around them to get what they want and need. Later, communicating is fun, frustrating, fascinating, and essential to work and play. This month students read a Tlingit legend in the oral tradition. In the halls, have students play with fantasy in phrases and ideas.

- ◆ Book of the month: *The Frog Princess: A Tlingit Legend from Alaska*, by Eric A. Kimmel and Rosanne Litzinger
- ◆ In the halls … Flights of fancy
- ◆ Inspiration from readers and writers
- ◆ Writing contest: Fantasy
- ◆ Family night: Favorites

## Book of the Month

In The Frog Princess: A Tlingit Legend from Alaska, by Eric A. Kimmel and Rosanne Litzinger, we feel the power of the oral tradition. "The village headman was a man of wealth and power. His daughter was one of the most beautiful girls in the Tlingit nation." After a suitor came to ask for her hand in marriage, she replied, "Marry you? Why I would sooner marry a frog from the lake!"

The tale illustrates the power of the oral tradition. Frogs have long been heralded for their connection to abundance, water, the Moon, and emotions. What we learn as readers is the tale of the headman's daughter and her transformation into the frog world. We also experience love, the power of happiness, and how one woman is able to transform the language of frogs.

We all learn to speak each other's languages by listening and sharing. By February, students are becoming adept at listening to each other's reading and writing and giving positive feedback.

## In the Halls ... Flights of Fantasy

Use the hall posters this month to help students explore the elements of fantasy. Keep the pattern of collecting ideas in the first week, followed by specific stories in the second week. In the third week, post the elements of story, and encourage students to give examples for each element from the fantasy stories they know and love. In the last add the hall poster to host student work.

- ◆ Week 1: Post a hall poster with magical words and pictures to inspire students to add their own
- ◆ Week 2: Post the names of stories from the fantasy genre
- ◆ Week 3: Post the elements of a story—characters, setting, problem, events, solution for students to add conversation bubbles about fantasy stories
- ◆ Week 4: Post fantasy stories/poems/essays by student authors/classes

## Share Readers' and Writers' Recommendations

This month you can begin asking for recommendations within a genre. Ask for fantasy recommendations with some science fiction added in for the older students. Post their recommendations, have them make them during morning announcements each week on the same day, and put them in the library with the book. The tradition of student and teacher recommendations should be well-established by now!

## Inspirational Highlights

Encourage teachers to integrate these quotations or others into their discussions with their classes. Discussing the quotations reminds everyone to think out loud about what they are doing, how they feel, why it is important, and that they can learn new strategies from each other.

*There are different rules for reading, for thinking, and for talking. Writing blends all three of them.* —Mason Cooley (b. 1927; U.S. aphorist; *City Aphorisms*, Twelfth Selection, New York, 1993).

*Long before I wrote stories, I listened for stories. Listening for them is something more acute than listening to them. I suppose it's an early form of participation in what goes on. Listening children know stories are there. When their elders sit and begin, children are just waiting and hoping for one to come out, like a mouse from its hole.* —Eudora Welty (b. 1909; U.S. fiction writer; *One Writer's Beginnings*, ch. 1, 1984).

*Learning is a result of listening, which in turn leads to even better listening and attentiveness to the other person.* —Alice Miller (20th century, German psychoanalyst and author; For Your Own Good, "Is There a Harmless Pedagogy?" Trans. 1983).

*Truly speaking, it is not instruction, but provocation, that I can receive from another soul. What he announces, I must find true in me, or reject; and on his word, or as his second, be he who he may, I can accept nothing.* —Ralph Waldo Emerson (1803–1882; U.S. essayist, poet, philosopher. Address, July 15, 1838, delivered before the senior class in Divinity College, Cambridge; "The Divinity School Address," reprinted in *The Portable Emerson*, ed. Carl Bode, 1946, reprinted 1981).

## Writing Contest: *Fantasy*

A Scottish writer, George MacDonald, is widely credited with writing the first fantasy novels, *The Princess and the Goblin* (1872) and *Phantastes* (1858). Many more familiar authors haves cited MacDonald as a major influence on their writing, including Mark Twain, J.R.R. Tolkien, Madeline L'Engle and C.S. Lewis. Popular fantasy novels include: C. S. Lewis's *Chronicles of Narnia* and Ursula K. LeGuin's *Earthsea* books, and J.K. Rowling's *Harry Potter* books. The genre is characterized by magic and supernatural elements in the nature and power of the characters, settings like lost worlds, and plots involving mystical turns of events.

## Family Night: *Favorites*

Set up the tables for this night with different topics of each table and one color crayon, marker, or stamp at each one.

### Topic Ideas

| | |
|---|---|
| Color | Shoes |
| Story | Adventure |
| Food | Weather |
| Piece of clothing | Store |
| Sport | Time of day |

Families get a blank book, folded and stapled like a 5" × 8" program with a construction paper cover. Kids and adults create the cover page and introduction together. At each table, there are books, stories, and poems about the topic. The adults write their favorite thing for the category—giving it a magical quality—and why on the left hand page, and kids write their favorite and why on the opposite page. They read them to each other. For example, "I love YELLOW because it's the color of the sun. Its heat and light make the Earth a beautiful place to live. Its magic is waking me up everyday. It makes me smile. I feel warm and happy when I see yellow. I always choose the yellow marker in games too."

# FEBRUARY WRITING CONTEST

## Fantasy

## Speaking and Listening—Telling a New Story

One of the best parts about writing stories is taking the reader with you on a journey into your imagination. We all have unique and wonderfully individual ideas. Share your originality with others.

For example you could pretend that you woke as an animal this morning. What would that animal be, what would it feel like, how would things be different, what would you do, where would you go? Write and illustrate a story about your adventure as an animal, or some other fantasy tale.

## Rules

You can make it as long or as short as you want
You are encouraged to add pictures
You are encouraged to be creative
You must have fun!

# Need Help?

## *What is imagination?*

Having a clear mental image of something new and different from your real experience.

## *Why become an animal?*

Being an animal gives you a different way to think, talk, move, and explore. Try walking like a crab, jumping like a deer, or talking like a cat.

## *What is fantasy?*

Fantasy is a genre that is based on magic and supernatural forms, lost worlds and mystical events. It is different than science fiction because there is little or no connection to what is actually possible and events are not explained in scientific terms. It is different than horror because it focuses on magic rather than fear.

# FAMILY NIGHT

## Favorites

*February \_\_\_ , 20\_\_\_\_*
*Save the date!*

Dear Parents, Families, Friends,

Our "Family Read-In" this month is all about *Favorites*. What is your favorite color? Story? Food? Sport? Animal? Emotion? Time of day?

Readers and writers are always looking to expand their ideas with rich detail. Being asked what your favorite is might be easy to answer, but to tell why, when, and how requires a lot more detail. To write about why it is your favorite, think about all the times you have seen it, how it made you feel, and give it a magical quality. For example, "I love YELLOW because it's the color of the sun. It makes me smile. I feel warm and happy when I see yellow. Its magic is waking me up every day."

You and your child will have the opportunity to make a book containing many of your favorite things; yours on the left-hand page and your child's on the right. To help with the descriptive writing there will be books, stories, and poems for ideas. Feel free to think out loud and ask others for their ideas. You will be able to take your new book home to read and share again and again.

Join us in describing your favorites, sharing ideas with your child(ren) and growing our culture of literacy in which we are interested in listening to each other.

Looking forward to seeing you there and hearing about your favorites!

# Chapter 9

# March: Reading to Learn, Writing to Understand

Why do things happen? From the toddler who can't stop asking "why" to the adult stuck in traffic, people ask "why" all the time. They not only ask why, they generate stories, hypotheses, and explanations for the things that happen. They often try to learn from what they believe are the causes of unpleasant effects to avoid them in the future or try to get good things to happen again. This month, students explore cause and effect in folktales, nonfiction, and in writing. You will want to have some nonfiction books on display for the month such as David McCauley's beautiful book, *The New Way Things Work* (1998); *How Science Works,* by John Farndon (1999); Neil Ardley's book, *How Things Work: 100 Ways Parents and Kids Can Share the Secrets of Technology* (1995).

- ◆ Book of the month: *Why Mosquitoes Buzz in People's Ears,* by Verna Aardema
- ◆ In the halls ... Cause and effect
- ◆ Inspiration from readers and writers
- ◆ Writing contest: *Folktales, cause, and effect*
- ◆ Family night: *Improvisation*

## Book of the Month

In *Why Mosquitoes Buzz in People's Ears,* by Verna Aardema with pictures by Leo and Diana Dillon, we learn about the buzzing habits of the mosquito and are drawn into the vivid world of legend and folklore. Mosquito spreads a lie to Iguana who wants nothing to do with her and her lie. He puts two sticks into his ears to block out Mosquito and in turn starts a series of events that ultimately lead to the death of one of Mother Owl's babies and a continuation of night.

King Lion said to the council, "So, it was the mosquito who annoyed the iguana, who frightened the python, who scared the rabbit, who startled the crow, who alarmed the monkey, who killed the owlet—and now Mother Owl won't wake the sun so that the day can come." This amusing African legend teaches through the rich tradition of a folktale. In the end, Mosquito learns not to lie but he adopts a much worse habit.

This African legend tells how people explain events in their world (perhaps this was an eclipse) and provides a springboard for getting students to read and write about why things happen and how they understand their world. The focus this month can be on nonfiction as well as fiction reading and writing with the structure of cause and effect.

## In the Halls … Cause and Effect

The goal this month for the hall posters is to develop students' language around cause-and-effect thinking. Even young children intuitively understand cause and effect—they chase pigeons in the park, scream to get attention, and bang toys on the floor to make loud noises. And yet, they do not always make the connection the other way. When they do something that gets them in trouble, they say, "I don't know how that happened!" This occurs in part because of how people think about cause and effect. When events occur together, they are often linked, such as a dog barking when a stranger approaches. It is assumed that the dog barked *because* the stranger approached because it happens some or even most of the time. When something happens out of the ordinary, people often try to think backwards to figure out the cause. But sometimes things occur together but don't cause each other. The key is to get students looking for evidence of cause and effect.

Keeping the pattern of week-by-week exploration of a concept, post some cause/effect relationships the first week to encourage students to post. In the second week, post some cause/effect relationships from stories with room for students to add more. In the third week, post the relationships from different kinds of cause/effect and have the students make conversation bubbles about *how* the cause and effect are connected.

♦ Week 1: Post a hall poster with cause/effect relationships to inspire students to add their own such as, the batter hit the ball for a home run, the boy pedaled hard to go fast, they have a hit song because teenagers love their music, everyone went outside today to enjoy the first warm day after winter.

- Week 2: Post cause/effect relationships from stories such as:

  Cinderella, who was no less good than beautiful, gave her two sisters lodgings in the palace

  The wolf huffed and puffed and blew the house down

  "Open, Sesame!" the captain said so plainly that Ali Baba heard him. A door opened in the rocks …

- Week 3: Post examples from physical, social, and biological cause/effect relationships for students to add conversation bubbles about *how* the cause/effect happens such as physically touching as in one ball hitting another, emotional cause/effect as in "she cried for joy when she saw him again" and social, "she went alone since all the others had gone on ahead."

- Week 4: Post stories/poems/essays by student authors/classes

## Share Readers' and Writers' Recommendations

Continue to inspire teachers and students to make recommendations from their love of books. In the morning announcements, read the most original ones and comment on how important it is to write them in creative ways, that you are not looking for a formula but for interesting experiments in reflection and persuasion.

## Inspirational Highlights

Electronic publishing on the Internet has added to the accessibility of print in our lives. We can read up-to-the-minute news and opinions on any event any—where in the world. Travelogues published only after trips were taken, are now published as the trips are happening. Individuals can publish their own adventures and ideas without the approval of anyone, making everyone an author who can be widely read.

If you have a school Web site, make your students' and teachers' "local quotes" available online as part of sharing your culture of literacy with the larger community.

*The illiterate of the 21st century will not be those who cannot read and write, but those who cannot learn, unlearn, and relearn.* —Alvin Toffler (b. 1928; U.S. author. "The Democratic Difference," pt. 1, ch. 2, *Powershift: Knowledge, Wealth, and Violence at the Edge of the 21st Century*, 1990)

*Some books are to be tasted, others to be swallowed, and some few to be chewed and digested: that is, some books are to be read only in parts, others to be read, but not curiously, and some few to be read wholly, and with diligence and attention.* —Sir Francis Bacon (1561–1626; English author, courtier, and philosopher)

*The test of literature is, I suppose, whether we ourselves live more intensely for the reading of it.* —Elizabeth Drew (1887–1965; Anglo-American author and critic, "Is There a 'Feminine' Fiction?" *The Modern Novel*, 1926).

*Any man with a moderate income can afford to buy more books than he can read in a lifetime.* —Unknown

*If the book we are reading does not wake us, as with a fist hammering on our skulls, then why do we read it … A book must be an ice axe to break the sea frozen inside us.* —Franz Kafka

## Writing Contest: *Folktales, Cause and Effect*

Folklore tries to capture the wisdom of a culture by explaining things through story, song, customs and traditions. Folktales fall into broad categories such as[1]:

- Cumulative tales that use repetition such as *The House that Jack Built*
- *Pourquoi* or "why" tales explain how something came to be, such as *How the Birds Got their Colors*
- Beast tales give animals human characteristics or anthropomorphize them such as *Three Billy Goats Gruff*
- Humorous tales in which a silly character makes mistakes, gets in trouble but in the end, all is well such as in *The Three Sillies* and *Fisherman and His Wife*
- Trickster tales such as coyote stories or *Anansi the Spider* and *Brer Rabbit*
- Realistic tales in which the characters are real people and do not have magic such as *Blue Beard* or *Dick Whittington and His Cat*
- Fairytales have magic and other supernatural characters and events such as *Cinderella* and *Beauty and the Beast*

---

1. http://www.bellaonline.com/articles/art38291.asp
   http://falcon.jmu.edu/%7Eramseyil/tradcarney.htm

Folktales can take the form of anecdotes, fables, jokes, parables, tall tales and urban legends. Encourage teachers and students to explore folktales of all different kinds and how they reflect their cultures.

The words that signal cause and effect are common conjunctions[2]:

| | | |
|---|---|---|
| Since | As a result | Because of |
| Because | Therefore | Due to |
| Consequently | For this reason | So |

For folklore and myth electronic texts see D.L. Ashliman's extensive Web site http://www.pitt.edu/~dash/folktexts.html

## Family Night: *Improvisation*

Invite several classes to plan to act out some of the folktales they have been reading for family night. Then do some improvisation with students acting out parts while another student reads the story aloud. At each table have some books and a few props. Encourage families to act out a story or poem for each other and then for another family. Wrap up the evening with a few volunteers performing their stories in front of the whole group.

---

2. http://lrs.ed.uiuc.edu/students/fwalters/cause.html

# MARCH WRITING CONTEST
## Cause and Effect in Folktales

Folktales are stories that are passed on by ordinary people telling them to each other. Often they are stories of animals who act like humans and struggle during the story to learn something or answer an important question. Ghost stories, jokes, legends, fables, fairy tales, myths, tall tales, and urban legends are different categories of folktales.

Some folktales try to explain how and why things happen through stories about the experience of characters. Create your own folktale that teaches the reader an important lesson through the character making a connection between a cause and an effect. ☺

## Rules
You can make it as long or as short as you want
You are encouraged to add pictures
You are encouraged to be creative
You must have fun!

## Need Help?

### How do I write a folktale?
Have an interesting main character and beginning, an important question to be answered by the main character, a series of events where the character makes a connection between a cause and an effect, and in the end answers the question.

### What are some examples of folktales?
*Aesop's Fables*, the *Beauty and the Beast*, *East of the Sun and West of the Moon*, just to name a few.

### What is a cause? What is an effect? What is the relationship between them?
A cause is the reason that something happens. An effect is what happens. The cause is the reason for the effect. The effect is the result of the cause. Words for cause/effect are "since, because, so, as a result."

# FAMILY NIGHT

## Improvisation

*March ___ , 20___*
*Save the date!*

Dear Parents, Families, Friends,

Our "Family Read-In" this month on is all about *Improvisation.* Bring your "drama queens" and "drama kings" and enjoy an evening of frivolity. Students have prepared short plays in which they act out a folktale read by their classmates. After the performance, you can try your hand at improvisation by acting out a story or poem and perhaps sharing your performance with the group.

Dramatic interpretation allows for great creativity and engages the whole child in the learning process. The physical action involved in acting brings words into the world. Acting goes beyond imagining or reading make-believe. Acting lets us try on new ideas and personalities like we try on different clothes. Please join us in an evening of acting out! ☺

Looking forward to seeing you there!

# Chapter 10

# April: Writing to Communicate Feelings and Ideas

The riddles of middles are the focus of much of this month. What happens in the middle of a story? Only the most important things! The conflict, rising action, crisis, and climax all happen in the middle. Even nonfiction can have a rhythm that builds to a critical amount or importance and then circles around quietly on the main ideas at the end. The writing contest is about the short forms of stories, plays, and poems that so often start with the action and refuse to resolve things at the end. Family night is about the feelings and actions portrayed in the illustrations that tell the story in picture books and enhance the telling in so many other forms of text. This month's activities include:

- Book of the month: *Waiting for Gregory,* by Kimberly Willis Holt
- In the halls … Caught in the middle
- Inspiration from readers and writers
- Writing contest: *Short story about feelings*
- Family night: *Art in literature*

## Book of the Month

In *Waiting for Gregory,* by Kimberly Willis Holt with paintings by Gabi Swiatkiwska, we live through Iris's changing feelings as she waits for her new baby cousin to arrive. "When will Gregory get here?" Iris asks her daddy. Iris asks the rest of her family to help her get a better idea of when her new cousin will arrive. Her grandpa tells her, "When the giant stork flies across the sky and drops him over your aunt's house." Her friend Lacey tells Iris that she can expect her new cousin after her aunt eats "a thousand chocolate-chip ice cream sundaes with sour pickles on top." Iris is so very excited about her new cousin that she plans a new activity to teach him with each new season. However, as the seasons pass so do her plans.

With each person she talks to, Iris is implanted with the seeds of new thoughts and begins to imagine new things that she and her cousin will do together. Once Gregory does arrive, Iris is ready to meet him and get started on their adventures. She discovers however, that he is "too tiny to fish, build a snowman, or ride a pony." As she learns new things about her cousin she creates new ways to interact with him. She is able to change her expectations and therefore adapt to the new situation.

Use this book to talk about how feelings are the stuff of stories and how we react to them. They remind us of our own lives, help us see other options and let us see how we often have similar feelings. This experience of communicating and connecting helps students feel more comfortable sharing their feelings in their writing.

## In the Halls … Caught in the Middle

In longer stories, the setting, characters and situation are introduced followed by some complication that introduces conflict that leads to a crisis and the climax and resolution. Short stories and other short forms like haiku poetry and one-act plays often start in the middle of the action. The text starts and you are left to figure out from the subtext what is going on and why. How people act toward each other and how they react to what is said begins to fill in the missing pieces. Then there is a critical incident, like someone gets shot or a secret is revealed which may lead to the central conflict. Use the hall posters this month to let students explore the what's in the middle of stories and how we signal the conflict, rising action, crisis, and climax.

♦ Week 1: Invite beginnings that start in the middle

She burst into the room crying

Begin in the Middle

*Post beginnings for a short story*

Not until that moment did she realize what had happened

He finally saw them coming

- Week 2: Post the four middle parts of a story to solicit words from students that signal each part.

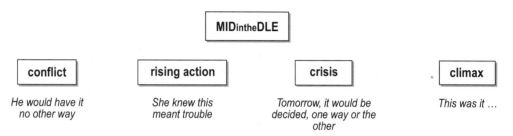

| MIDintheDLE | | | |

| conflict | rising action | crisis | climax |

| He would have it no other way | She knew this meant trouble | Tomorrow, it would be decided, one way or the other | This was it … |

- Week 3: Post the four middle parts in a grid so students can tell the four parts for a familiar story

| STOmiddlesRY |

| CONFLICT | RISING ACTION | CRISIS | CLIMAX |
|---|---|---|---|
|  |  |  |  |
|  |  |  |  |
|  |  |  |  |

| CONFLICT | RISING ACTION | CRISIS | CLIMAX |
|---|---|---|---|
|  |  |  |  |
|  |  |  |  |
|  |  |  |  |

- Week 4: Post original short stories or one-act plays by students

## Share Readers' and Writers' Recommendations

Make this month's recommendations about "shorts." Ask teachers and students to recommend their favorite short stories, one-act plays, and short poems. Have a storytelling time at lunch, in the morning, or after school, for students and teachers to tell their favorite stories. Set a goal that everyone in the school will learn at least one story to tell.

## Inspirational Highlights

Feel free to modify the quotations and just add, "adapted from" the author and work. You may wish to make the quotation shorter or substitute easier words, like "joy" for "felicity" or "happy" for "satisfied." Continue to encourage teachers to use the quotations in their classes during the week, giving students ways to respond, and collecting "local quotes."

*The first time I read an excellent work, it is to me just as if I gained a new friend; and when I read over a book I have perused before, it resembles the meeting of an old one.* —James Goldsmith (1728–1774; Anglo-Irish author, poet, and playwright)

*To feel most beautifully alive means to be reading something beautiful, ready always to apprehend in the flow of language the sudden flash of poetry.* —Gaston Bachelard (1884–1962; French scientist, philosopher, and literary theorist; "A Retrospective Glance at the Lifework of a Master of Books," *Fragments of a Poetics of Fire,* 1988, trans. 1990)

*Writing is the action of thinking, just as drawing is the action of seeing and composing music is the action of hearing. And all that is inward must be expressed in action, for that is the true life of the spirit and the only way we can be continually discarding our dead and mistaken (sinful) selves and progressing and knowing more.* —Brenda Ueland (1891–1985; U.S. author and writing teacher; *If You Want to Write,* 2nd. ed., ch. 3, 1938).

*[The pleasures of writing] correspond exactly to the pleasures of reading, the bliss, the felicity of a phrase is shared by writer and reader: by the satisfied writer and the grateful reader, or—which is the same thing—by the artist grateful to the unknown force in his mind that has suggested a combination of images and by the artistic reader whom his combination satisfies.* —Vladimir Nabokov (1899–1977; Russian-born U.S. novelist and poet; Interview, 1964)

## Writing Contest: *Illustrated Short Story About Feelings*

Plan with the faculty to introduce the children to Caldecott award winning books, and to engage them in analyzing what makes these books winners. This month, encourage as many children as possible to write illustrated short stories to share with their families on Family Night. Allow the children to cut and paste pictures, help each other draw, and even make computer art. All illustration styles, techniques, and media are encouraged. From Shel Silverstein's playfully illustrated books to the classics, illustrations are part of the story.

Since short stories emerged from oral traditions, they depend heavily on the illustrations to tell the story. Details that young children could not grasp through language come through in a picture. Illustrated stories are wonderful *reading-together* books because the adult and child can read the pictures together since the child can get so much information on his or her own from a picture.

This month's writing contest focuses on writing short stories about feelings. This approach often helps to create the single focus that is characteristic of short stories. It can build on the discussions of cause and effect from the previous month in describing an incident that caused strong feelings and reactions. Modern short stories are especially fun for children to explore writing (or dictating in the early grades) since they often begin abruptly in the middle of the action. They may also end abruptly, making the reader feel as if he or she dropped into a situation, like opening the door of a room full of people who just continue what they are doing as if you hadn't entered.

## Family Night: *Art in Literature*

At family night, you can have some children read their stories and show the pictures. You will want to take digital pictures of the pages so they can be projected from the computer for all to read. Other students' stories can be displayed along with Caldecott winners. After having a few (brave) children read their stories to the whole group, have other children reading simultaneously to their families at the tables. For those families who do not have original works to read, provide the Caldecott books, crayons, markers, and paper for them to write and illustrate a story on the spot. Feature these "hot off the press" stories throughout the evening to create excitement.

# APRIL WRITING CONTEST

## Illustrated Short Stories About Feelings

We all have lots and lots of feelings every day. Most days, we experience many different feelings too. Not everyone feels the same way about things as you do. Some love baseball, others love dance, and still others love reading. Some feelings are big and some are small. Some feelings you like to have and others you don't.

Choose a feeling and write a short story about that feeling. You can include the color(s) you become, how it makes others feel, what makes you feel this way, and what other feelings are similar to the one you chose. Find pictures or illustrate your story. Your stories will be shared at Family Night this month!

## Rules

You can ask for help from anyone
You must have pictures!
You are encouraged to be creative
You must have fun!

# Need Help?

## *What are some feelings I might have?*

Angry, anxious, beautiful, brave, calm, capable, childish, confident, defeated, determined, embarrassed, excited, foolish, frantic, frustrated, glad, guilty, happy, hopeful, humble, hurt, hysterical, insecure, inspired, irritated, jealous, joyful, loved, mean, misunderstood, nervous, optimistic, overwhelmed, powerful, relaxed, sad, satisfied, suspicious …

## *Can you give me an example?*

Sure! Anger feels like a hot, humid, summer day with lots of bugs and no ice for my drink, no shade in site, and the town pool closed. That day I was really angry …

## *What is a short story?*

Short stories can be fiction or nonfiction. They are short (of course) and get to their point quickly. They are simple, usually about one event in one setting in a short period of time with only a few characters.

# *FAMILY NIGHT*

## Art and Literature

*April ___ , 20 ___*
*Save the date!*

Dear Parents, Families, Friends,

Our "Family Read-In" this month is all about *Art and Literature.* As you can see by the wonderful artwork in the halls around the school, we love art. There is a special acknowledgment in literature called the Caldecott Award, which is named in honor of nineteenth-century English illustrator Randolph Caldecott and is awarded annually to the artists of the most distinguished American picture book for children. Students have chosen books that they feel represent this level of artistic value and have created their own works as well.

This is a very special night for your children. They will be talking about their work and artistic representation and interpretation from their chosen literary work. Some children will be sharing their favorite illustrated book while others will be sharing original work. You will be able to visit many children and view their work. I know that they all look forward to sharing with you.

Artistic impression is a valuable way to grow understanding. At home, I encourage you to sit and draw, color, and create with your child(ren). Enjoy this window into a child's mind through the use of art in literature.

Enjoying the viewing.

# Chapter 11

# May:
# Weaving Our Stories Together

This month is about how stories reflect real life. Nonfiction takes so many forms, entertaining and teaching us. Nonfiction is both precise and creative, analytical and expressive. Capturing real life accurately is a challenge rewarded by the knowledge that someone will learn from what you write. This month's activities include:

♦ Book of the month: *If You Give A Mouse A Cookie,* by Laura Joffe Numeroff

♦ In the halls … Nonfiction

♦ Inspiration from readers and writers

♦ Writing contest: *Nonfiction and partnerships*

♦ Family night: *Nonfiction*

## Book of the Month

In *If You Give A Mouse A Cookie,* by Laura Joffe Numeroff illustrated by Felicia Bond, a young boy sitting along an the edge of his yard offers a cookie to a mouse passing by. "If you give a mouse a cookie, he's going to ask for a glass of milk. When you give him the milk, he'll probably ask you for a straw." After you have read him a story, he has taken a nap, you have cleaned up after him, he draws a picture and hangs it on the fridge, and you give him another glass of milk, "he's going to want a cookie to go with it."

Stories often take on a life of their own. What starts out as a simple idea can grow into an elaborate tale—diverse and complex. Often, the first step is the hardest one when beginning the journey as an author. Joffe Numeroff illustrates how a simple idea can grow into a great story of adventure. Students want to explore, and can begin to see reading and writing as a way to have fantastic adventures where their imaginations are freed and their spirts soar.

## In the Halls … Nonfiction

Use the hall posters to help students explore nonfiction as a genre this month. In week 1, prompt them to post what fiction is and what it is not. In week 2, students can list their favorite nonfiction books. In week 3, they can list their favorite sources of nonfiction, and in week 4, post their own short nonfiction.

- Week 1: Post, "Nonfiction is …" and "Nonfiction is not …"
- Week 2: Post, "What are your favorite nonfiction books?"
- Week 3: Post, "Where do you find nonfiction?" (books, magazines, posters, encyclopedias, newspapers, manuals, textbooks, poems)
- Week 4: Post students' nonfiction works

## Share Readers' and Writers' Recommendations

Ask for recommendations for nonfiction this month. Encourage classes to have book talks about books on their favorite topics.

## Inspirational Highlights

Autobiographies and biographies are wonderful forms of nonfiction. They give us the inside story, from the person's own hand or those who are close observers. Revisit them as a form of nonfiction in this month's quotes.

*Reading any collection of a man's quotations is like eating the ingredients that go into a stew instead of cooking them together in the pot. You eat all the carrots, then all the potatoes, then the meat. You won't go away hungry, but it's not quite satisfying. Only a biography, or autobiography, gives you the hot meal.* —Christopher Buckley (U.S. author; A review of three books of quotations from Newt Gingrich, "Newtie's Greatest Hits," *The New York Times Book Review*, March 12, 1995)

*Reading while waiting*
*for the iron to heat,*
*writing, My Life had stood—a Loaded Gun—*
—Adrienne Rich (b. 1929; U.S. poet; "Snapshots of a Daughter-in-Law" (l. 43–45) in *The Norton Anthology of Poetry*, Alexander W. Allison et al., Eds., 3d ed., 1983, W. W. Norton & Company).

*We pass the word around; we ponder how the case is put by different people, we read the poetry; we meditate over the literature; we play the music; we change our minds; we reach an understanding. Society evolves this way, not by shouting each other down, but by the capacity of unique, individual human beings to comprehend each other.* —Lewis Thomas (1913–1993; *The Medusa and the Snail*, 1979)

*No one is truly literate who cannot read his own heart.* —Eric Hoffer (1902–1983; U.S. philosopher; *Reflections on the Human Condition*, 1973)

## Writing Contest: *Partnerships, Nonfiction*

In his essay, *Variations on a Theme of Putting Nonfiction in its Place*,[1] Robert Root offers the following:

1.  The written expression of, reflection on, and/or interpretation of observed, perceived, or recollected experience;

2.  A genre of literature made up of such writing, which includes such subgenres as the personal essay, the memoir, narrative reportage, and expressive critical writing and whose borders with other reality-based genres and forms (such as journalism, criticism, history, etc.) are fluid and malleable;

3.  The expressive, transactional, and poetic prose texts generated by students in college composition courses; and

4.  Not fiction.

Nonfiction is a rich form of expression, spanning cultures, and time periods. It offers wonderful opportunities for the use of expressive language and creative organizations to entice and interest the reader in the topic at hand. Nonfiction is oh so much more than the encyclopedia or the textbook. At dif-

---

1.  Presentation Text, CCCC, March 2002 by Robert Root, Central Michigan University. http://www.chsbs.cmich.edu/robert_root/Background/Variations.htm

ferent ages, children devour different topics, but they invariably crave information about whatever they are interested in at the time, from dinosaurs to music to sports.

Some basic organizations of nonfiction text are described in chapter 15: descriptive, problem and solution, time sequence or order, compare and contrast, cause and effect, and question and answer.

This month's contest focuses on writing fiction with a partner or about a partnership as part of the theme of community and culture.

## Family Night: *Reading to Learn*

It's funny because fiction and nonfiction are the two broad categories of writing, but nonfiction has to be true. Even if it is a little bit untrue, as in telling a story about a time in history and making up details through dialog, makes it historical fiction, not embellished nonfiction. But there is a nod to the emphasis on truth by putting "historical" first, rather than fictional history, which means something entirely different.

For this family night, have fun exploring nonfiction in all its forms. Have on hand travelogues, book reviews, content books, how-things-work books, newspapers, magazines, and diaries, as well as the children's nonfiction pieces from the writing contest.

Post some questions for families to discuss as they choose and read together a nonfiction source:

- What do you want to learn from reading?
- What did you learn?
- Why do you believe it to be true?
- How does the way it is organized help you learn?
- Does this make you want to learn more? What do you want to learn now?

For writing activities, have some tasks for the family to write directions for, such as peeling an orange or making a peanut butter and jelly sandwich. After the directions are written, one person reads them and the other person follows them very literally. For example, "Put the peanut butter on the bread" results in putting the jar on top of the bread. You know this is great fun if you have done it and at the same time it focuses people's attention on the importance and difficulty of describing a sequence of steps very carefully. Precise language is a cornerstone of nonfiction.

# MAY WRITING CONTEST

## Nonfiction and Partnerships

When we are young, we learn about sharing and working together. This learning never stops and is always important. Working together is helpful because you get to combine your ideas and build with each other. Think of the great partnerships in history: the Wright Brothers, Lewis and Clark, Watson and Crick, the Leakeys. These are real life stories of partnerships that produced great things. Partnerships are one way we work together in real life.

Find a partner and tell each other some true stories. Choose one to write together, or each write your own. You can also write about partnerships. Remember to illustrate your story. If you wrote it together, plan to tell it as a team. Your story can be about any situation you like.

### Rules

You can make it as long or as short as you want
You are encouraged to add pictures
You are encouraged to be creative
You must have fun!

## Need Help?

### Who are Watson and Crick and the Leakeys?

Working together, Watson and Crick determined the structure of DNA. The Leakeys—Louis, Mary, and their son, Richard—helped determine how humans evolved.

### What is important to remember when working together?

Respect each other, think how you can help your partner learn, help when you can, do your part, and remember you are in this together.

### What is nonfiction?

Nonfiction is an account of something presented as fact. It may not be fact, but it is presented as fact rather than fiction.

# FAMILY NIGHT

## Nonfiction: Reading to Learn

*May ___ , 20___*
*Save the date!*

Dear Parents, Families, Friends,

Our "Family Read-In" this month is all about *Nonfiction*. Come and explore our wonderful collection of nonfiction material.

Bring your favorite source of nonfiction—a newspaper, journal, magazine, or manual. What do you read to learn more?

Do you write any nonfiction? Directions, instructions, or descriptions? If so, bring those too. If not, try your hand with some fun nonfiction writing activities you can do as a family.

We hope you have enjoyed our family nights this year. This will be our last one, so please be sure to come. We have a special present for you for summer literacy activities.

See you there!

# Chapter 12

# June and July: Read On

This month the theme is "Read On" to encourage students and families to plan to read all summer long. If you are still in school this month, you will probably not have time for a family night since there will be end of the year events like concerts and graduation. If you do have time for one, a book fair is a good idea so families can buy or exchange books for the summer. Have a corner with shoeboxes that students can make into mini-bookshelves by covering or decorating them. Have another table for making bookmarks with construction paper, stamps and ribbon or yarn. Invite the public librarian to come to be sure everyone has a current library card and to remind everyone of summer hours at the library. If you have a local bookseller or storyteller, invite them too!

- ◆ Book of the month: *Magic Beach*, by Crockett Johnson
- ◆ In the halls ... Illusions, allusions, foreshadowing and mystery
- ◆ Inspiration from readers and writers
- ◆ Writing contest: *Read on, Mystery*

## Book of the Month

In *Magic Beach*, by Crockett Johnson, we share the adventures of a boy and a girl who discover the power of words on an enchanted beach. "I'm tired," said Ann. "We should have stayed at the cottage and read a story.... It's more fun to do something yourself instead of reading about it," said Ben. "I wouldn't mind if we were in a story," said Ann., "Because people in stories don't go around all day looking for an old shell. Interesting things happen." And for Ann and Ben, they do.

The importance of continued reading for children over the summer is undeniable. What we read continuously shapes who we are, our experiences, and our ideas. *Magic Beach* was originally written to be an "I Can Read" book in the late 1950s but was dismissed by critics because it was too difficult for children. By the same author as *Harold and the Purple Crayon,* this book lets children see how they can draw themselves into the future.

## In the Halls ... Illusions, Allusions, Foreshadowing and Mystery

What builds suspense? Footsteps on the stairs, a stranger arriving late at night, the sound of a door knob turning, a box without a key—all build suspense. Use this month's hall posters to have students explore the mystery writer's craft. In week 1, collect ways to build suspense like the events above. In week 2, have students post pictures of settings that create mood with one-liners. These can be drawings or pictures from magazines or newspapers, or printed from an online source. In week 3, have fun with, "It looked like ... but it was really ..." Following the pattern, post student stories that use illusions, allusions, foreshadowing, and mystery in week 4.

- Week 1: Post "Ways to Build Suspense"
- Week 2: Post "Mysterious Moods" to collect pictures of settings
- Week 3: Post "Red herrings" to collect ways to mislead the reader
- Week 4: Post student stories

## Share Readers' and Writers' Recommendations

Encourage students and teachers to recommend their best "summer" book ever. Send the list of the top recommendations for the year for primary and intermediate students home in a newsletter to encourage summer reading.

## Inspirational Highlights

Get students and teachers thinking about things that were once mysterious to them and are not anymore. Have them share their "quotations" about the wisdom they now have like these authors:

*What we become depends on what we read after all of the professors have finished with us. The greatest university of all is a collection of books.* —Thomas Carlyle (1795–1881; Scottish author, essayist, and historian)

*It is books that are a key to the wide world; if you can't do anything else, read all that you can.* —Jane Hamilton, The Book of Ruth

*It is well to read everything of something, and something of everything.* —Henry Peter, 1st Baron Brougham and Vaux Brougham (1778–1868; Scottish Whig politician; Speech, January 29, 1828, to the House of Commons.

*The books we read should be chosen with great care, that they may be, as an Egyptian king wrote over his library, "The medicines of the soul."* —Paxton Hood (1820–1885; English nonconformist clergyman)

## Writing Contest: *Read on, Mystery*

Summer is still a wonderfully mysterious time for many children and their families. Perhaps it comes from having more time to spend together, more opportunity to explore the neighborhood or new places, or the time and space for them to discover themselves. There are new, as well as old friends when children sign up for classes or camp, and there is always learning, for that is what children do.

Maybe this month's writing contest will get some students hooked on mysteries so they will be looking for the mysterious in their summer.

The elements of a good mystery are a character who is the mystery solver, something that is lost, some place to hide it, and some hint that will result in finding it.

# SUMMER WRITING CONTEST
## Mystery in Fact and Fiction

From "the case of the missing" to "whodunit" mysteries are the kind of stories you just can't put down. They keep you on the edge or your seat trying to figure out what happened, or how the mystery will be solved. Even nonfiction writing uses mystery to draw us into the search for the last of an endangered species, or that one piece of information that will solve a problem.

This is your chance to try your hand at writing a mystery. Try starting with the missing object or idea, and think of it as the missing piece of a puzzle. Map out all the other pieces and reveal them one by one so your reader finally is in on the solution.

## Rules
You can make it as long or as short as you want
You are encouraged to add pictures
You are encouraged to be creative
You must have fun!

## Need Help?

### What advice can you give?
Have the last piece of the puzzle be the biggest clue to the mystery.
Write about a setting or topic you know well so your clues are very detailed.
Think about red herrings—bits of information that mislead readers.

### Do I need to read some mysteries?
Definitely! Read several short stories to get ideas for how to organize your story. Don't be afraid to use someone else's story as a model and just change the content.

### What make s a good mystery?
A good mystery has a character who is the mystery solver, something that is lost, some place to hide it, and some hint that will result in finding it.

# Final Reflection

In this section, activities great and small have been presented for you to try. Dip into them, follow them religiously, or read through them on Sunday nights to plan your week. But however you use what you find here, take time to reflect each week on how what you have done has affected those in your school community, how your actions have strengthened the culture of literacy. This will increase your wisdom and with it, your confidence as a literacy leader.

**Month:** *Template*   **Theme:** _____   **Book of the month:** _____

| Monday | Tuesday | Wednesday | Thursday | Friday |
|---|---|---|---|---|
| Inspiration | Faculty meeting to plan activities for book of the month | Announce/post book recommendations | In the halls … | |
| Easel/morning announcement inspiration | Launch book of the month for school | | In the halls … | Announce writing contest |
| Easel/morning announcement inspiration | | Teacher recommended book | In the halls … | |
| Easel/morning announcement inspiration | | Student recommended book | In the halls … | Recognize winners of writing contest |
| Easel/morning announcement inspiration | Post book of the month responses | | In the halls … **Family Night** | |

**Month**: *August*  **Theme**: *Getting ready to learn*  **Book of the month**: *Oh, the Places You'll Go!* by Dr. Seuss

| Monday | Tuesday | Wednesday | Thursday | Friday |
|---|---|---|---|---|
| Inspiration | Faculty meeting—discuss book of month | Announce/post book recommendations | In the halls … *Beginnings* | Writing contest |
| *The man who doesn't read good books has no advantage over the man who can't read them.* | Launch *Oh, the Places You'll Go* | | *Favorite beginnings* | Announce **Goal-setting and the quest** |
| *There is a great deal of difference between an eager man who wants to read a book …* | | Teacher recommended book | *Excerpts from books* | |
| *Play gives children a chance to practice what they are learning…. They have to play …* | | Student recommended book | *What beginnings signal* | Recognize winners of **Goal-setting and the quest** |
| *There are books so alive that you're always afraid that while you weren't reading …* | Post responses to *Oh, the Places You'll Go* | | Student work Family night: *Talking about what you read* | |

**Month:** *September*    **Theme:** *Becoming a Learning Community*    **Book of the month:** *Stone Soup, by Marcia Brown*

| *Monday* | *Tuesday* | *Wednesday* | *Thursday* | *Friday* |
|---|---|---|---|---|
| Inspiration | Faculty meeting—discuss book of month | Announce/post book recommendations | In the halls … *Figurative Language* | Writing contest |
| *One ought, every day at least, to hear a little song, read a good poem, see a fine picture …* | Launch *Stone Soup* | | *Favorite figures of speech* | Announce *A sense of community, descriptive essay* |
| *Reading furnishes the mind only with materials of knowledge; it is thinking that makes …* | | Teacher recommended book | *Excerpts from books* | |
| *Learning and teaching should not stand on opposite banks and just watch the river flow …* | | Student recommended book | *Meanings of figures of speech* | Recognize winners of *A sense of community, descriptive essay* |
| *Language is the soul of intellect, and reading is the essential process by which that …* | Post responses to *Stone Soup* | | Family night: *Reading together* | |

**Month:** October    **Theme:** Beginning Where You Are    **Book of the month:** *Walk On! A Guide for Babies of All Ages,* by Marla Frazee

| Monday | Tuesday | Wednesday | Thursday | Friday |
|---|---|---|---|---|
| Inspiration | Faculty meeting—discuss book of month | Announce/post book recommendations | In the halls… **Connections** | Writing contest |
| *Reading made Don Quixote a gentleman. Believing what he read made him mad.* | Launch ***Walk On! A Guide for Babies of All Ages*** | | *Favorite segues* | Announce ***Journeys, time sequence, autobiography*** |
| *People say that life is the thing, but I prefer reading.* | | Teacher recommended book | *Excerpts from books* | |
| *It would be worth the while to select our reading, for books are the society we keep…* | | Student recommended book | *What segues signal* | Recognize winners of ***Journeys, time sequence, autobiography*** |
| *Never read a book through merely because you have begun it.* | Post responses to ***Walk On! A Guide for Babies of All Ages*** | | *Student work* Family Night: ***Read to each other*** | |

**Month:** November   **Theme:** Becoming Authors   **Book of the month:** *Click, Clack, Moo Cows That Type,* by Doreen Cronin

| Monday | Tuesday | Wednesday | Thursday | Friday |
|---|---|---|---|---|
| Inspiration | Faculty meeting—discuss book of month | Announce/post book recommendations | In the halls … *Painting pictures with words* | Writing contest |
| *Reading a book is like re-writing it for yourself.... You bring to a novel, anything you....* | Launch *Click, Clack, Moo Cows That Type* | | *Favorite imagery* | Announce *Poetry* |
| *Writing and reading is to me synonymous with existing.* | | Teacher recommended book | *Excerpts from poems with imagery* | |
| *Like dreaming, reading performs the prodigious task of carrying us off to other worlds …* | | Student recommended book | *What imagery brings to mind* | Recognize winners of *Poetry* |
| *Don't join the book burners. Don't think you're going to conceal faults by concealing ….* | Post responses to *Click, Clack, Moo Cows That Type* | | *Student work Family night: Interpreting what you read* | |

**Month:** December   **Theme:** The Gift of Reading   **Book of the month:** *Wild About Books*, by Judy Sierra

| *Monday* | *Tuesday* | *Wednesday* | *Thursday* | *Friday* |
|---|---|---|---|---|
| Inspiration | Faculty meeting—discuss book of month | Announce/post book recommendations | In the halls.... *Alike or different* | Writing contest |
| *When I read a book I seem to read it with my eyes only, but now and then I come across...* | Launch ***Wild About Books*** | | *Fun with similarities and differences* | Announce ***Book reviews*** |
| *If you can read this, thank a teacher.* | | Teacher recommended book | *Excerpts from books with comparisons* | |
| *In a real sense, people who have read good literature have lived more than people who...* | | Student recommended book | *Descriptions of situations, people, places and things through compare and contrast* | Recognize winners of ***Book reviews*** |
| *Properly, we should read for power. Man reading should be man intensely alive. The...* | Post responses to ***Wild About Books*** | | *Student work* Family night: ***Poetry for dessert*** | |

**Month:** January  **Theme:** Celebrating Progress  **Book of the month:** *The Daddy Mountain*, by Jules Feiffer

| Monday | Tuesday | Wednesday | Thursday | Friday |
|---|---|---|---|---|
| Inspiration | Faculty meeting—discuss book of month | Announce/post book recommendations | In the halls.… *Plotting with seven basic plots* | Writing contest |
| *True ease in writing comes from art, not chance…* | Launch *The Daddy Mountain* | | *Seven plots* *Favorite stories* | Announce *Celebrating progress* |
| *Writing is an exploration. You start from nothing and learn as you go.* | | Teacher recommended book | *Books for the seven plots* | |
| *Reading maketh a full man; conference a ready man; and writing an exact man.* | | Student recommended book | *What always happens in each plot* | Recognize winners of *Celebrating progress* |
| *With one day's reading a man may have the key in his hands.* | Post responses to *The Daddy Mountain* | | *Student work* Family night: *Grandparents as storyteller* | |

**Month:** February **Theme:** Speaking and Listening **Book of the month:** *The Frog Princess: A Tlingit Legend from Alaska*, by Eric A. Kimmel

|  | Monday | Tuesday | Wednesday | Thursday | Friday |
|---|---|---|---|---|---|
| Inspiration |  | Faculty meeting—discuss book of month | Announce/post book recommendations | In the halls… *Flights of fancy* | Writing contest |
| *There are different rules for reading, for thinking, and for talking. Writing blends …* |  | Launch *The Frog Princess: A Tlingit Legend from Alaska* |  | Magical words and pictures | Announce *Imaginative, fantasy* |
| *Long before I wrote stories, I listened for stories. Listening for them is something more …* |  |  | Teacher recommended book | Stories and books in the fantasy genre |  |
| *Learning is a result of listening, which in turn leads to even better listening …* |  |  | Student recommended book | Elements of a story —the fantasy version | Recognize winners of *Imaginative, fantasy* |
| *Truly speaking, it is not instruction, but provocation, that I can receive from another …* |  | Post responses to *The Frog Princess: A Tlingit Legend from Alaska* |  | Student work Family night: *Favorites* |  |

**Month:** March   **Theme:** Reading to Learn   **Book of the month:** *Why Mosquitoes Buzz in People's Ears*, by Verna Aardema

| *Monday* | *Tuesday* | *Wednesday* | *Thursday* | *Friday* |
|---|---|---|---|---|
| Inspiration | Faculty meeting—discuss book of month | Announce/post book recommendations | In the halls… **Cause and effect** | Writing contest |
| *The illiterate of the 21st century will not be those who cannot read and write, but those …* | Launch ***Why Mosquitoes Buzz in People's Ears*** | | *Cause/effect relationships* | Announce ***Folktales, cause, and effect*** |
| *Some books are to be tasted, others to be swallowed, and some few to be chewed …* | | Teacher recommended book | *Excerpts from stories showing cause and effect* | |
| *The test of literature is, I suppose, whether we ourselves live more intensely for the …* | | Student recommended book | *Different kinds of cause and effect* | Recognize winners of ***Folktales, cause, and effect*** |
| *Any man with a moderate income can afford to buy more books than he can read in a lifetime.* | Post responses to ***Why Mosquitoes Buzz in People's Ears*** | | *Student work* Family night: *Improvisation* | |

**Month:** April   **Theme:** Writing to Communicate Feelings and Ideas   **Book of the month:** *Waiting for Gregory*, by Kimberly Willis Holt

| Monday | Tuesday | Wednesday | Thursday | Friday |
|---|---|---|---|---|
| Inspiration | Faculty meeting—discuss book of month | Announce/post book recommendations | In the halls… ***Caught in the Middle*** | Writing contest |
| *The first time I read an excellent work, it is to me just as if I gained a new friend…* | Launch ***Waiting for Gregory*** | | *Beginnings that start in the middle of the action* | Announce ***Cause and Effect in Folktales*** |
| *To feel most beautifully alive means to be reading something beautiful, ready always…* | | Teacher recommended book | *Signals for conflict, rising action, crisis and climax* | |
| *…writing is the action of thinking, just as drawing is the action of seeing and composing…* | | Student recommended book | *Middles in familiar stories* | Recognize winners of ***Cause and Effect in Folktales*** |
| *[The pleasures of writing] correspond exactly to the pleasures of reading, the bliss…* | Post responses to ***Waiting for Gregory*** | | *Student work Family night: **Art in literature*** | |

**Month:** May  **Theme:** Weaving Our Stories Together  **Book of the month:** *If You Give A Mouse A Cookie*, by Laura Joffe Numeroff

| Monday | Tuesday | Wednesday | Thursday | Friday |
|---|---|---|---|---|
| Inspiration | Faculty meeting—discuss book of month | Announce/post book recommendations | In the halls … *Nonfiction* | Writing contest |
| *Reading any collection of a man's quotations is like eating the ingredients that go into…* | Launch *If You Give A Mouse A Cookie* | | Nonfiction is … Nonfiction is not … | Announce *Partnerships, nonfiction* |
| *No one is truly literate who cannot read his own heart.* | | Teacher recommended book | *Favorite nonfiction books* | |
| *Reading while waiting for the iron to heat, writing, My Life had stood—a Loaded Gun—* | | Student recommended book | *Sources of nonfiction* | Recognize winners of *Partnerships, nonfiction* |
| *We pass the word around; we ponder how the case is put by different people, we read …* | Post responses to *If You Give A Mouse A Cookie* | | *Student work Family Night: Nonfiction—Reading to Learn* | |

**Month:** June & July   **Theme:** Read On   **Book of the month:** *Magic Beach*, by Crockett Johnson

| *Monday* | *Tuesday* | *Wednesday* | *Thursday* | *Friday* |
|---|---|---|---|---|
| Inspiration | Faculty meeting—discuss book of month | Book recommendations | In the halls… Illusions, Allusions, Foreshadowing and Mystery | Writing contest |
| *What we become depends on what we read after all of the professors have finished…* | Launch *Magic Beach* | | *Ways to build suspense* | Announce ***Read on, mystery*** |
| *It is books that are a key to the wide world; if you can't do anything else, read all that you can.* | | Teacher recommended book | *Mysterious moods* | |
| *It is well to read everything of something, and something of everything.* | | Student recommended book | *Red herrings* | Recognize winners of ***Read on, mystery*** |
| *The books we read should be chosen with great care, that they may be, as an Egyptian…* | Post responses to *Magic Beach* | | *Student work* | |

# Part 2: Study Guide

The principles behind the month-by-month activities are presented in these chapters for your review and reflection. Each chapter begins with *Questions to Ponder Before Reading.* You may use these as an individual reader, or as a group for discussion in grade-level study groups, cooperative peer groups, in a class on literacy, or as a faculty. Suggestions for *Reflection* appear at the end of each chapter to help you apply and extend what you have read and/or to add to the month-by-month activities in the plan book.

# Chapter 13

# How Do You Start Telling the Story of Your School?

<table>
<tr><td>

**Questions to Ponder Before Reading**

◆ What story would you tell about the school culture where you learned to read?

◆ How did you learn to read? Who is part of your story?

◆ Who is the storyteller in your school, family, or community? Who captures, recalls, and retells events that define the group? How and why do they do it? How does the group react?

◆ How do you feel about storytelling? Do you do it? Love it? Lose patience with it?

</td></tr>
</table>

A community grows through its stories. Although a story is usually written by one person, good stories speak to all our lives. How often have we been like Milo in the *Phantom Tollbooth*[1] lying in bed and wanting to travel to the lands beyond, spinning a tale of adventure that is missing in our own lives? Or, how many times have we found ourselves in trouble through no fault of our own like the brothers in Chris Van Allsburg's *Zathura*,[2] and wished we could figure our way out of it by working with our friends or family? Stories start with experience. From there, they can become fanciful or practical, or simply tell what happened. In a school, stories build a sense of community. We become more respectful of each other as we hear each other's stories. Those stories create bridges between people. They give people a way to share, and to be curious about each other, rather than judgmental.

---

1. *The Phantom Tollbooth*, by Norman Juster, 1988.
2. *Zathura*, by Chris Van Allsburg, 2002.

# Story Starters

You can be the town crier in your school. Tell about what is happening in classrooms, in parent meetings, or in the community. For example, I remember a "literacy market" we had in sixth grade. In the *Phantom Tollbooth*, Milo goes to Dictionopolis, a city of words. In the book, every morning people go to market to buy the letters and words they need for the day, so we had our own literacy market. Each student chose a letter, then collected words that used that letter in a prominent way such as Mississippi for "i." After a couple of weeks of collecting, we brainstormed how we could buy and sell words. The students decided we needed food for each booth, something symbolic of the letter, or connected with one of the words with that letter. The "x" booth had pretzels, the "b" booth had butter cookies, the "s" had tasty little sausages. Like planning any good potluck dinner, students negotiated a balanced menu and prepared their dishes before market day arrived. By the time families arrived, each booth had its letter prominently displayed with lots of words and pictures connected with that letter. Five students gave an overview of the story. Three others set the stage for the market, by reading from the book and handing out sentence strips and plates. Shoppers had to create a balanced meal for themselves *and* a good sentence.

The event became a tradition after one of the parents wrote up the event for the newspaper with the article from the previous year serving as publicity. Norman Justus became a favorite author with the sixth graders being asked to be read aloud to the family, especially younger brothers and sisters. The math teachers decided to hold a market day for numbers in "Digitopolis" and the social study teachers asked students to compare the lure of "the lands beyond" to the explorations in the ancient world. The excitement and intense participation of the students spread throughout the school and the community because people were talking about it—telling the story of their participation.

Another way to start a story is to begin with one idea and ask other people to chime in and complete the other parts. Find the seed ideas that are ready to burst open. Nurture ideas by spreading the word of a good idea and the potential for a good story if others join in. For example, the physical education teacher had a guest modern dance company one day a week for four weeks. The principal asked her to talk about the group to the entire faculty to look for connections. In physical education, students had been learning groups of movements, so the objective was to have the students see how groups of movements could have a language and carry meaning as well as add up to skills such as shooting a basket or hitting a ball. The music teacher saw an opportunity for students to score and accompany the dances the students created in physical education. The language arts teacher thought some of his classes could describe the dance movements, while others could write lyrics, and still others could report on the performances for the school paper with interviews with teachers, students and dancers.

By the time the dance company came, 10 classes were involved in the production, and an assembly and evening event had been scheduled for the performance of student-choreographed pieces with original scores, lyrics, and accompaniment. In science classes, students watched video and wrote about the physics, anatomy, and physiology of dance. In language arts classes, some students wrote sequels to the "story" of the dance. Others wrote retrospectives from 15 years in the future, remembering the event and telling how it had influenced their choices in the intervening years. Younger students wrote thank you notes to the dance troupe, the student performers, choreographers, and composers.

The physical education teacher told the story of the dance troupe and her vision of what could happen. The other teachers each added to that story in the making and then again in the telling of what happened. Once the activities began, the students added their voices to shape the story. Through the creation and the telling, another school tradition was born. A rich learning environment was built on collaboration and continual attention to listening, piggybacking on each other's ideas, telling the story as it unfolded, and finding audiences for retelling through performance and writing.

## Tell the Community's Stories

Everyone has stories to tell about what they envision, what they care about, and what they want to do with students. As a school leader, you can help these stories emerge to create a sense of community through sharing experiences and language. For some people, you will need to tell their story, endorse it, and invite others to talk with them about it and build on it. For others, you will need only to notice what they are doing, make connections with other people in the school and bring the collaboration out in the open for the whole faculty. Your expectations matter, so if you expect your faculty, staff, students, and families to be supportive of each other, to be creative, and to build on each others' ideas, they will. The following sections describe some practical strategies for bringing out the stories in your school community. As you read them, you will have other ideas. Jot them down at the end of this section or go ahead and put them on the calendars in the plan book.

## Spread the Word

You can celebrate the successful practices in the school through stories in the principal bulletin, at faculty meetings, or even in a student-written newspaper. As a school leader, you visit all the classrooms, know the strengths of all the teachers, and know all the students. Jot down story ideas as you move throughout the building and send out your team of student reporters to write a few paragraphs about best practices for the school newsletter. Use these in your reports to the district office and board to celebrate progress. Carry a camera and take pictures of interesting centers, displays of student work, or effective classroom management ideas. Share these at a faculty meeting, getting the teachers to talk about the how and why of what you captured. The ritual of elevating these small moments through recognition makes the person proud, and everyone else more interested in hearing about the things going on in the building.

> *A culture is an active living phenomenon through which people jointly create and recreate the worlds in which they live.*
>
> —Gareth Morgan

## Monthly Writing Contest

Sponsor a writing contest once a month to get other storytellers to be heard. This is a fun way to ensure that writing is going on throughout the building on a regular basis. Once the faculty agrees on a writing rubric (see a sample below), students can write and revise based on peer and teacher feedback. Encourage students to write about how they are learning to write. "Learning" stories don't have to be the only kind of stories, but they are important to develop a culture where everyone is reflecting on how they are learning.

Have each class submit their best two writing pieces, then have the teachers choose the top three pieces for each grade level. This gets teachers analyzing writing samples together and discussing the rubric. You rank them, and announce the first, second, and third place for each grade level. Feature them at the monthly family night, with the authors there to read excerpts if possible. Be sure to put them on display for reading by everyone throughout the next month, then house them permanently in the student author section of the library. Don't forget the all important comment pages in the back of each book. This will keep the authors coming back to see what their readers have said. See if you can get your local newspaper to publish the top stories for all the grade levels, then publish the second and third place stories in your school newsletter. You may also want to have the stories read aloud at lunch time.

> ## March Writing Contest
>
> ### *Cause and Effect in Folktales*
>
> Folktales are stories that are passed on by ordinary people telling them to each other. Often they are stories of animals who act like humans and struggle during the story to learn something or answer an important question. Ghost stories, jokes, legends, fables, fairy tales, myths, tall tales and urban legends are different categories of folktales.
>
> Some folktales try to explain how and why things happen through stories about the experience of characters. Create your own folk tale that teaches the reader an important lesson through the character making a connection between a cause and an effect.

## Lunchtime Literacy Activities

Jamie Turner, principal of Fairhaven Elementary, has talent shows, a reading corner, and math contests in the cafeteria at lunch time. The reading corner has a donated couch and some comfy chairs with student-authored books beautifully displayed on a tiered stand like you would find in a store or at a book fair. For those who want to escape the noisy cafeteria, this spot just outside the door in the hall is the perfect place to sit. Other students may be sharing a talent like juggling, skateboarding, or drumming in the cafeteria. They sign up for 5-minute blocks to perform for their schoolmates. These times are very popular and often lead to new collaborations for future performances. Once a week, Turner has math or word puzzle contests with prizes. Lunchtime is more civilized and the stories of student accomplishments are told through their performances. Through making books available and creating a ritual for sharing, they are building a culture in which students listen well to each other.

# What makes my writing worth reading? Writer's Rubric

## Student Rubric with Conferencing Questions for the Author to Use with a Reader

| | Focus<br>What is the point of the story? | Content<br>What does the reader know from reading what I wrote? | Organization<br>How did I tell the story? How did I organize it? | Style<br>What pictures did my writing paint in the reader's mind? | Conventions<br>What do I need to proofread for? |
|---|---|---|---|---|---|
| 4 | The reader knows what my point is about, the topic, and why I think that. | I choose the most interesting and important ideas to tell the reader in an interesting, fun way to make my point. | I chose to organize it the way I did to be interesting and easy to read. | People can tell that a piece of writing is mine by how I write. | Anyone can read and understand my writing because I use correct spelling, punctuation, and grammar. |
| 3 | I make one big point about the topic or idea in the prompt. There are a lot of smaller ideas to support the big idea. | I know what I am talking about and the reader does too after they read what I wrote. It makes my point. | I tell what I know like a story with a beginning, middle, and end connected with transition words. | My readers feel like I am talking to them and they are part of what is happening. I use lots of interesting words and phrases. | When I reread what I wrote, I corrected the spelling, punctuation, and grammar. |
| 2 | I chose ideas that go together and tell why I think they go together. | I collected a lot of ideas and used the best ones to make my point. | I thought about how to tell the story so it would make sense to the reader. | I write like I talk. I want readers to understand what I write. | I asked a classmate to read my writing and ask me questions about what wasn't clear to her. |
| 1 | I write some ideas about the topic that come into my mind as I write. | I write about some things I have heard about the topic. | I write down what I think in the order I think of it. | I tell what happened in just a few sentences. | I write a bunch of ideas instead of complete sentences. I spell words like I hear them. |

| Nonscorable: blank, illegible, incoherent, insufficient | Off-prompt: readable but does not respond to prompt |
|---|---|

# Stories About Learning to Read

A monthly writing contest topic could be, "How I Really Learned to Read." Students interview a family member about how the student themselves, or a family member learned to read. It may be that someone *really* learned to read when they discovered mysteries and couldn't get enough of them, or they wanted to build a rocket so they read a lot about it, and then read some more. One of my students' parents said that her son really learned to read off the pizza box that they seemed to buy a couple of times each week. He loved pizza and would point at the box all the way home. His 8-year-old sister would read the words on the box that he pointed to, so he would point some more and she would read some more. One day at dinner, he pointed to the words on the box and read them one by one, "fresh, hot pizza." Of course, at 3 years old, he had memorized the words, rather than decoding them, but he was definitely making the connection between words for something he loved and the print on the box. So, at some level, his mom was right about how he learned to read.

For the contest, each student author conducts the interview with someone about how he learned to read, then writes the story. Then s/he writes about the writing of the story. Students understand this idea from viewing the backstory, or behind the scenes clips on DVDs. The writing of the story behind the story is the metacognition that gets the author thinking about *how* things went and consolidating an understanding that will make it easier to remember and apply what s/he learned to writing the next piece. Ask the local paper to write a story about learning to read, featuring excerpts from the students' stories and their behind the scenes stories. Compile the top two stories for each grade level into a book that goes into the student author lending library on how people learn to read. Have the students read their stories at a family night early in the year. Send the authors into the younger grades so children and families see how many different ways and at different ages people learn to read. Don't forget the reader remarks pages at the end of the book. Create audiences and opportunities for student authors to be heard and read.

The writing contest topics in the month-by-month activities are:

♦ August: Goal setting, the quest
♦ September: Community, descriptive essay

- October: Journeys, time sequence, autobiography
- November: Poetry
- December: Book reviews, compare/contrast
- January: Celebrating progress, problem, and solution
- February: Fantasy
- March: Folktales, cause, and effect
- April: Short story about feelings
- May: Partnerships, nonfiction
- June and July: Read on, mystery

## Summary

In a culture of literacy, reading and writing are not subjects, but an integral part of every day. They are what people talk about, what they share and how they communicate. Think of the school as a book group or a writer's group. Model the power of story in everything you do and invite others to tell their stories, to listen well, and to build on them out of each other's ideas. When everything relates to books, students both seek and write them.

What ideas can you add to the calendar from this chapter? If you haven't done so already, jot down some ideas, or make notes about how you will adapt the ideas from this chapter that are already on the calendar.

## Reflection

Telling the stories of how people learned to read is fun and fascinating for everyone since learning to read is such a milestone on the way to reading to learn. What are other literacy stories that could be told from your school and community? What do people love to read? What are they learning from what they read? How did people learn to write? What are they writing about? How do they write? Where do they write? What is helping students to learn to read? What strategies are helping readers read nonfiction to learn? What are some favorite Internet sites? Magazines? Newspapers? Why? What other questions about literacy do you want to ask in your school community that will elicit stories of growth and success?

# Chapter 14

# What is a Culture of Literacy

## Questions to Ponder Before Reading

♦ What do you remember about the presence of books and the use of language in school?

♦ Who do you know who loves words and language? How does this love affect what they do and say, how and where they spend their time, and who and what they surround themselves with?

♦ What are the rights and responsibilities of students in learning to read and write well?

♦ What are the rights and responsibilities of teachers in learning to read and write well?

♦ What are the rights and responsibilities of administrators in learning to read and write well?

♦ What are the rights and responsibilities of families in learning to read and write well?

What is a culture of literacy? Words, words, words. You know a culture of literacy when you walk into it. There are words everywhere. Words with pictures, letters, essays, and quotations are everywhere. Words are used carefully, cherished, and celebrated. Teachers listen to students. Students listen to each other. Yes, that's right, students listen to each other. They see that teachers listen to each other. People care to listen and listen to show they care. They value each other's experience and learn through dialog. They have conversations about things they have read, things they have done, and what they are learning. Language clearly connects people to each other, to ideas, and to learning. Language is used positively and respectfully to understand and nurture each other's learning.

> *People care to listen and listen to show they care.*

## Books, Books and More Books

The space in the school and classrooms invites reading and writing. There are books everywhere. There are nooks and crannies to read in with comfortable chairs and rugs. There are student-written books displayed for other students to read. Every book has pages in the back for readers to leave notes for the author. A student-written newspaper reviews books and interviews student authors. There are many rituals around books in which both children and families can participate.

Everyone reads independently at least 30 minutes in and out of school every day. Children see adults and each other reading. All classrooms have libraries of books children can and want to read. All children have growing home libraries. Adults read to, with and in front of children. Books written by children, teachers, and parents are displayed prominently and read by everyone in the community. Author nights feature student authors.

## Language is Fun

In a school arranged this way, people see language as complex, nuanced, powerful, and fun. In a culture of literacy, people talk, read and write just for fun. They share what they think, what they read, and what they write as a way to learn from each other. People write about upcoming events to let everyone know about them, and they write about the events afterwards to include those who were unable to come and celebrate the participation of those who did by telling the story.

Word games and puzzles, word play, and poetry make words fun. Scrabble tournaments, old-fashioned spelling bees, limerick contests, and poetry readings are on the calendar. Every month there are ways for families and students to have fun with words and many roles to take in the culture of literacy.

## Language is Productive

When a school culture supports literacy development in all its children, everyone believes that reading and writing are the stuff of everyday living.

Everyone is committed to each child making progress in their skills and strategies, their love of reading, and their confidence in writing. They are committed to surrounding children with books, magazines, stories, and songs written and read by themselves and others. Classrooms are rich in language, full of wonder, and discussion. Teachers are focused on how their students are learning the connections between talk, thinking, and the printed word.

## Using Language Well is Everyone's Right and Responsibility

In a school culture built on literacy, everyone has rights and responsibilities. The International Reading Association published a list of rights of children in January 2000 that inspired the following bill of rights. Post these in prominent places, put them in your student handbook, and share them with parents at family nights. Survey your students to see if they are exercising their rights and living up to their responsibilities.

*Everyone has access to many writers and everyone can be a writer who is read.*

You are teaching your students what it means to have the United States Constitution guarantee every child a free public education, and with it, the right to learn to read, write, and compute. On another level, you are teaching students that rights come with the responsibility to exercise those rights to improve yourself and contribute to the society that protects your rights. This is a powerful way to talk about the privilege and at the same time the challenge of learning to understand and use the printed word. It was not so long ago that the printed word belonged only to the elite. Now, like then, the word opens up worlds to those who master it. The difference is that many more children have access to learning to read and write, and technology has increased access to information. Everyone has access to many writers and everyone can be a writer who is read.

When a whole school or district commits to a bill of rights like this one, they also commit to supporting each other in living up to the rights and responsibilities contained in it. As Booker T. Washington put it, *"Few things help an individual more than to place responsibility upon him, and to let him know that you trust him."*

## Student Rights and Responsibilities

Students have the right to have books they can read, people to talk to about what they are reading, and time to make connections between what they are reading and their own ideas. They have the responsibility to think out loud about the strategies they use and to learn new strategies from their teachers, parents and other students. Students have a responsibility to talk and write about what they are reading and to actively and consciously use language to make sense of what they are reading.

| Student Rights |
| --- |
| ♦ Have access to books that they can read independently so they can read for pleasure and to learn. <br> ♦ Have people to talk to about what they read so they can reflect on its importance for them. <br> ♦ Have a chance to think about what they read so they can integrate it into what they know, feel, and do. |

| Student Responsibilities |
| --- |
| ♦ Learn new strategies to improve their reading so they can be more and more successful in reading more and more complex materials. <br> ♦ Write about what they read to make connections to their ideas, other texts, and learn ways of expressing themselves through writing. <br> ♦ Think out loud about what and how they are reading so other students, teachers, and parents can help them to improve. |

Teachers may want to do their own versions of these rights and responsibilities such as this short version for primary students:

| Student Rights | Student Responsibilities |
| --- | --- |
| ♦ Have books you can read by yourself. <br> ♦ Have time to think about what you read and write. <br> ♦ Have people you can talk to about what you read and write. | ♦ Learn new strategies. <br> ♦ Write about what you read <br> ♦ Think out loud about how you read and write |

You can make these rights and responsibilities come alive by featuring a few students each week talking about their favorite strategies. If you have a school blog, students can post their favorite strategies each week. Connect these rights and responsibilities to the typical "reading club" activity, where students are recognized on a wall for reading 25, 50, 75 and 100 books or more. Without access to books they would not achieve these goals and by reading regularly they are being responsible students.

# Teacher Rights and Responsibilities

Just as students need access to books and people to talk with about what they are reading and writing, teachers have a right to diagnostic tools and instructional materials at different levels. Another teacher right is to have regular professional development and time to share/plan with colleagues so they develop a deep understanding of how children learn to read and write and are able to apply what they learn to teaching specific children.

| *Teacher Rights* |
| --- |
| ◆ Understand how children learn to read and write. |
| ◆ Have the tools and training to help them make specific diagnoses about what children are good and at and what they need. |
| ◆ Have easy access to books and instructional materials at multiple levels. |
| ◆ Have regular professional development and time to share and plan with colleagues. |

With these rights in place, teachers have the responsibility to model good reading and writing, instruct children in groups and individually, and collect samples that show students' progress over time. They need to build in time for students to become thoughtful readers and writers by reflecting on what and how they are learning.

| *Teacher Responsibilities* |
| --- |
| ◆ Model good reading and writing. |
| ◆ Use a variety of instructional groupings: Model good reading for children in large groups, teach them specifically what they need in small groups, conference with children individually to track their progress and hear how they are thinking and feeling about their reading and writing. |
| ◆ Schedule time for students to reflect on what and how they are learning. |
| ◆ Collect samples that show student progress over time. |

These rights and responsibilities are the core of creating a culture in the classrooms and throughout the school that supports children learning to read and write well.

## Administrator Rights and Responsibilities

Administrators too need to have a deep understanding of how children learn to read and write. Such an understanding informs each interaction with teachers and students and allows the administrator to model effective skills and strategies in countless small ways. It allows the administrator to actively support immersion in literacy activities with careful attention to skill and strategy development. The administrator has the right to expect all students to learn the strategies they need to be successful readers and writers, and to expect all faculty to provide instruction at a student's level to help them be successful and improve. The administrator has the right to expect all families to support literacy development in their children through reading and talking with their children every day.

| *Administrator Rights* |
| --- |
| ♦ Understand how children learn to read and write. |
| ♦ Expect all faculty and staff to contribute to every child learning to read and write and to using reading and writing to learn, communicate, and have fun. |
| ♦ Expect all families to read with their children every day. |
| ♦ Allocate the resources to buy books for the library, the classrooms, and special events. |
| ♦ Expect all students to learn these strategies to be successful readers and writers. |

The administrator can rally the whole school around events that involve families, students, and faculty across all the grade levels. The administrator and the school management team are responsible for budgeting for books and other materials, for special events and professional development. Often, the principal or literacy specialist can lobby for additional support through the district office, or write grants to supplement the local school budget. They may be able to garner local support for particular programs or events. For example, an elementary principal in a Title 1 school asked a local store to provide a bicycle for their reading raffle. Every time 100% of the students in a class brought in their signed, "I read with my child for 15 minutes tonight" forms, everyone in that class was entered into the bike raffle. Of course there were other prizes, especially books, but it was the potential of owning the bike that kept participation high.

| *Administrator Responsibilities* |
| --- |
| ◆ Model good reading and writing strategies. |
| ◆ Provide in-service for teachers. Lead monthly discussions about literacy topics. Arrange for teachers to have time to talk and plan. Provide diagnostic tools to help teachers make instructional decisions for students. Expect teachers to help each child develop new, more powerful skills and strategies for reading and writing. |
| ◆ Involve parents and community members in actively supporting literacy development with clear expectations, strategies, ideas and encouragement. |
| ◆ Fill the school with books, poems, and posters about reading and writing. Make the library the hub of the school. |
| ◆ Emphasize literacy with whole-school activities. For example, have "stop everything and read times," and lead whole-school book read-ins. |

More than any single person, the principal sets the expectations for how the school looks—what goes in the halls and around the school. Every principal expects teachers to post things in the hall, but the principal focused on literacy leads the way with information about books, writing samples and author information, and expects teachers to display and change student writings and drawings that shows how they are making sense of how to use language.

# Family/Caregiver Rights and Responsibilities

Everyone can contribute in big and small ways to children learning language. It is as simple as reading and writing more, and as complex as figuring out what a child understands and doesn't understand about how language works. The key is to have constant conversations about the strategies readers and writers use, and the wonderful world of ideas and experience that reading opens up. In a culture of literacy everyone is a reader and writer, everyone is learning, and it is completely okay to be exactly where you are in that process.

| *Family/Caregiver Rights* |
|---|
| ◆ Understand how they can help their children learn to read and write. |
| ◆ To know how their children are doing as readers and writers from their children's teachers. |
| ◆ Have access to good books and other materials for children to read and to read to them. |

| *Family/Caregiver Responsibilities* |
|---|
| ◆ Read with their children every day. Read aloud to children. Model good reading and writing. |
| ◆ Listen to children read. Talk with them about what they are reading. Encourage them to tell stories and to write them down. Discuss movies, television, and Internet "stories." |
| ◆ Provide books for children to read at home, from the library, school, or purchased. |

## Summary: Envision a Culture of Literacy

When I think out loud about what I believe, it comes out something like this:

*In this country, we believe that all our children can and have the right to learn to read and write. We value language-rich classrooms, full of wondering and discussion by students where teachers are focused on how their students are learning the connections between ideas, print, and oral language. In our district, we are committed to providing our teachers with the support and materials they need to teach every child to read and write so they are confident and proficient.*

*While children are busy in our classrooms, their business is communicating, learning to read, and reading to learn. They do many different kinds of activities but they are focused on using those activities to learn the strategies that good readers and writers use. Strategies are something everyone can learn with practice and coaching, so we focus on strategies rather than ability because every child can learn to use new strategies.*

*We want children to cherish language. Words are precious in our personal and social lives. We want our children to use words to understand their experience and to share it with others. The author C.S. Lewis once said that we read so we know we are not alone. Perhaps we write so that others can share in our personal experiences. We want our students to use their words to add meaning to their lives. We want them to become authors, storytellers, friends, family and community with shared memories and experience. We want them to know each other through the pictures they paint with their words, the questions they ask, and the dreams they have. We want them to be affirmed, challenged, and inspired by the thoughts of others that are made visible through words.*

# Reflection

How would you describe what you value and how it connects to what your goals and activities are? Take a moment to write about what you care about and how you are translating your vision into what you do.

# Chapter 15

# How Does Language Work?

## Questions to Ponder Before Reading

♦ Do you think of language as simple or complex? Why?

♦ If you were asked to explain how the English language works to a nonnative speaker, what would you tell him or her?

Although we seem to take it for granted, it is truly amazing that children learn to speak and understand a complex language within the first two years of their lives. They use language to make their needs, desires, and thoughts known to get what they need and want. In the United States, children expect to be initiated into the mysteries of reading by the end of first grade. If they don't learn to read in first grade, most will learn by the end of second grade. Unfortunately after second grade, those who do not learn to read may put more energy into pretending they can read or avoiding it altogether. Like speaking, most children will learn to read if they are supported rather than pressured. It is incredibly painful to not know how to read in our society.

Even many expert readers cannot explain how they uncovered the mysteries of the written word. We don't remember the frustrations of learning to speak; what we couldn't understand or how other people didn't seem to understand us. If we learned to read easily, we may know even less about how we learned to read. Parents are often very surprised that their children struggle to read, or don't progress with other children of the same age. In fact, it is perfectly normal for children to learn to read anywhere between ages 4 and 8. They progress in fits and starts, and sometimes leaping to fluency rather than grow into it.

And yes indeed, there are mysteries in our language and how we learn it. Here are a few principles that will help you, students, and others who work with them to become powerful and proficient users of the language. First and foremost, you can let them know that they are hardwired to learn language, that the English language is complex, but has base elements that they can learn to recognize and use in writing as well as they do in speaking.

## Children are "Hardwired" to Learn Language

Children have everything they need to be able to learn to read and write just like they learned to speak. They will learn in much the same way as they learned to speak, by using the language for a purpose. Reading books at their levels about subjects they are interested in will accelerate reading mastery. Having their stories written down so they can read their own words over and over again builds the connection between what they say and the written word. Just as when they learned oral language, they need to be immersed in a culture where everyone, including them, is reading and writing all the time.

## English Does Not Always Follow the Rules

Because we teach children rules and patterns, they sometimes mistakenly believe language is regular, when, in fact, it is not. The rules apply some of the time, but not all the time. Some words are pronounced like they look, others are not. Some words are spelled just like they sound; others are not. Students should always rely on what makes sense to their ears and to their minds. Spelling rules are especially tricky because we have agreed on a set of rules that don't always fit the way words are pronounced. We pronounce words based on their origins and our regional accents. "Sounding out" a word often helps because when children get part of word, they can figure out what it is from the rest of sentence or passage and from what they know about the world. If they rely solely on the way the letters strung together would sound, they will be disappointed and frustrated. If they do not know any letter sounds, they will be unable to pronounce the word well enough to recognize it. The important thing is for children to understand that the rules are really helpful but they only work some of the time. With this mindset, children will value the rules, and try them out, and they won't be frustrated when they don't work.

## Written English is Made Up of Five Basic Elements

*Letters* that have shapes and sounds make up *words* that have parts and go together to make *sentences* that tell who does what when that make up *paragraphs* that tell more of a *story* with details over time and combine to make up stories that have plots. The basic elements of the English language are:

- Letters: 26 different letters with 44 sounds
- Words: We use 100 words 50% of the time
- Sentences: 4 types[1]
- Paragraphs: 7 types[2]
- Stories: 7 basic plots[3]

The New York Public Library once ran a full-page ad in the *New York Times* with the 26 letters of the alphabet running across the middle of the page from left to right. The caption at the bottom read, "Come see what people have done with these." Children need to know that the core elements of language are finite; it makes learning to read and write seem so much more manageable.

## Letters and Sounds

With 26 letters and 44 sounds, the numbers of sounds and letters don't always match. Consider "mat" which has 3 letters and three sounds; m-a-t. "Match" also has three sounds but it has 5 letters; m-a-tch. Students need to expect that sounds and letters don't match up. That way they won't be disappointed or frustrated. They will be more willing to play with words, experiment with how they might sound when you look at them in print, and search for clues in the context.

## Four Types of Sentences

The four types of sentences correspond to the feelings, ideas, and needs children have so they already know the content and form of them, but they need to express themselves in writing and recognize the intent of other authors. They can read aloud to attach the emotion to the words. Below are the types of sentences with examples about a sudden snowstorm.

- Declarative sentences make statements and describe

  *It started snowing around 4:00 A.M. so by the time we woke up at 7:00 A.M. it was 6 inches deep.*

1. http://www.emints.org/ethemes/resources/S00000357.shtml
2. http://www.longleaf.net/ggrow/modes.html
3. http://denisdutton.com/booker_review.htm

- Imperative sentences express needs, command attention, or action

  *"We need to get out of here quickly so we can get to the ski resort before the roads are closed," my husband said.*

- Interrogative sentences make requests, ask for things, help, or information

  *"What will we do if we get snowed in at the ski resort?"*

- Exclamatory express excitement

  *"We'll have a terrific time skiing today and tomorrow with no crowds!"*

## Seven Types of Paragraphs

The seven types of paragraphs are also familiar to even very young students. Anchoring them in the meaning children already make in their lives makes using them in print so much easier.

- Narration: Children tell stories almost as soon as they can talk about who does what and why. Their stories have sequence, present events, and often have setting, conflict, and a resolution.

- Exposition: Children explain things. They even have a sense of trying to be credible by giving reasons for their explanations. Piaget tells about asking 5-year-olds where Lake Geneva came from. Some children said people made it, others said rain made it, but what was remarkable was that most of the children had reasons they shared with conviction.

- Definition: Children don't naturally use the dictionary perhaps in part because they understand that the best definitions come from the meaning found in the world. When children ask someone for a definition, they may get stories, what it is not, synonyms, and sentences putting it in context.

- Classification: Children learn early on to sort shapes and colors, to make patterns, and compare things on different dimensions. With prompting they can talk about how things compare and fit into categories.

- Description: The best descriptions focus on actions and that's what children use in early simple sentences. It takes awhile for them to be able to describe what the reader needs to see instead of sharing their egocentric focus.

- ◆ Process analysis: Children can describe how to make a peanut butter and jelly sandwich, how to tie their shoes, and various other processes they are learning so describing them in detail becomes fun and surprisingly challenging.

- ◆ Persuasion: "Please, please, please!" Children cajole, plead, and throw tantrums to persuade others to give them what they want. Persuasion is a survival skill so learning to recognize and write a paragraph focused on persuading someone to do something will serve them well.

- ◆ Just as with the meaning behind sentences, children understand and use the basic types of paragraphs in their lives. This gives them the most important piece in being able to use the written word for their purposes.

# Texts: Fiction and Nonfiction

I remember my fifth grade teacher, Mrs. Moore, saying that there were only seven basic plots. I couldn't believe it! All the stories in the world had only seven plots? It was too good to be true. I was afraid to believe it. Throughout all these years of reading, I think about those plots and wonder if the story I'm reading fits one of them. While the list of seven is an unnecessary oversimplification for me as an adult, as a child, it was like getting in on a very big secret on how stories are written.

In this section, some basic text structures will be introduced for your consideration and use. You will no doubt modify the lists of structures to meet your needs. The key is to identify the structures and help children consciously use them to understand what they read and to us them when they write. The goal is to make them a systematic part of instruction and assessment. Seven basic plots, six informational text organizations, and multiple genres are discussed.

Children need to read both narrative and nonnarrative texts and to note the characteristics of the subcategories of texts. Children enjoy nonnarrative texts about topics of interest to them, or as a way to explore new ideas. When asked, they are able to talk about the structure of nonnarrative texts. For example, they notice, can describe, and even can use structures, such as in a mystery where there is a character who solves mysteries, a suspect, a missing object, person, or piece of information, and a way to discover what is missing.

# Seven Basic Plots

In the same way that the types of sentences and paragraphs are familiar to children through their experience, the seven basic plots are a starting point for students to think about the plots in their lives and to connect them with what they read and what they write. Christopher Booker[4] identifies the following seven plots:

♦ Overcoming the monster: The hero fights, escapes death, and finally saves the world from evil. In stories such as *The Epic of Gilgamesh*, *Little Red Riding Hood*, and James Bond films, the conflict ends in victory. In their own lives, children conquer the monster under the bed and fears of loud noises, crowds, and strangers.

♦ Rags to riches: *Cinderella*, *The Ugly Duckling*, and *David Copperfield* are stories that tell of modest, downtrodden characters whose special talents or beauty are finally revealed to the world. This is the stuff of imaginary play where every child is a hero.

♦ The quest: Features a hero, normally joined by sidekicks, traveling the world and fighting to overcome evil and secure a priceless treasure. Young children's quests are immediate and within view but they are nevertheless pursued with vigor such as collecting cards, dolls or coins or being the best at games.

♦ Voyage and return: From *Alice in Wonderland* to Goldilocks to *The Time Machine*, the characters either choose a voyage or fall into a strange world that they must figure out how to return from. Children love the story of Hansel and Gretel's clever idea of bread crumbs and try it out on their own mini-adventures.

♦ Comedy: Confusion reigns until at last the hero and heroine are united in love or things work out for the star. Children grow up on cartoons where comedy reigns. Their heroes are funny, slapstick, never die, and always win in the end. Children are naturally silly. They pretend they can fly, hit a ball to the moon, and rocket power their skateboards.

♦ Tragedy: Portrays human overreaching and its terrible consequences. The bad guys always lose in children's stories and movies. They are

4. Booker, C. (2005). *The seven basic plots: Why we tell stories.* New York: Continuum.

bigger than life, supremely overconfident, and inevitably fail. From the Big Bad Wolf to wicked witches, these characters end up in trouble. In real life there are bullies who get their "come-up-ins."

♦ Rebirth: Centers on characters such as Dickens's Scrooge or Snow White, telling the story of their transformations. Young children already believe anything can change at any time: toys can come alive, road runner is smashed but comes back to life.

## Six Nonfiction or Informational Organizations

Knowing how nonfiction text is organized also aids in comprehension. Hoyt and Therriault (2003)[5] identified five core text structures. Harvey (1998)[6] added a sixth. They are given here with examples about eye twitching.

1. Descriptive: *Sometimes my right eye twitches, not so much that you would notice, but I can feel it. It feels like the eyelid is jumping a half an inch, when really it is moving very little.*

2. Problem/solution: *When my eye starts to twitch I know I am overtired and need to get more sleep. As soon as I get a good night's sleep, or even a long nap, I wake up without the twitch.*

3. Time/order (i.e., sequence): *First, I don't get enough sleep. Then I don't recognize it and try to keep going without resting. Not long after that, the eye twitch starts.*

4. Comparison/contrast: *Some people's eyes hurt when they are overtired. Others are like me and have a twitch.*

5. Cause and effect: *When I am overtired, my right eye twitches uncontrollably.*

6. Question and answer: *What can you do when you have a twitching eye? Think about how much sleep you have had and plan to get more.*

The key to comprehension and clear writing is expecting the text to have a familiar structure rather than reading each new text as if it were the only one of its kind. Armed with the expectation that there will be a pattern in the text, the student is able to read strategically, looking for the characteristics of the text associated with the genre, type of plot, or organization. This text knowledge builds on students' understanding that structure matters in language, from sentences, to paragraphs, to fiction, and nonfiction texts. Just as

5. Hoyt, L., Mooney, M., & Parkes, B. (Eds.). (2003). Part 1: Bringing informational texts into focus. In *Exploring informational texts: From theory to practice* (p. 1). Portsmouth, NH: Heinemann.
6. Harvey, S. (1998). *Nonfiction matters: Reading, writing, and research in grades 3-8.* Portland, ME: Stenhouse.

the role of the word in the sentence adds so much meaning from context, and the role of a sentence in a paragraph signals its level of generality as a main or supporting idea, the section, act, or part of a story lets the reader expect a certain kind of information or activity.

## Genres

A genre is a specific category of text, marked by a distinctive style, form or content. Texts in a genre share similar content, ways of unfolding, key types of characters and often, styles. From their experience, children often understand these categories, such as knowing that a mystery will be solved, a horror story will have aberrant characters or events as well as normal people, a short story may be unresolved, and a sports piece will be about the game as well as the people.

A short list of genres might include the following, although some lists are much longer, and new genres are appearing like Web pages and blogs in the electronic environment. As students "discover" genres, they can create their own lists with descriptions of what to expect from the text structure.

| | | |
|---|---|---|
| Adventure | Horror | Thriller |
| Fantasy | Mystery | Poetry |
| Science Fiction | Humor | Real Life |
| Romance | Sports | Short Story |
| Historical Fiction | Supernatural | Fairy tale |
| Legend | Autobiography | Biography |

## Reading is All About the Cues

Children need to think of themselves as detectives. Their discovery tools are the three cueing systems to be successful readers: meaning, structure/ syntax and visual cues. The most powerful cueing system is the meaning system. When they read, they need to be thinking about what they are reading (getting meaning) and seeing each word/phrase as part of a larger structure (syntax). If they get stuck on a word, they will use their letter/word part knowledge to "solve" the word (visual cues), or get close enough to what it might so that it makes sense within the meaning and structure of the larger passage.

When we confess to children that our language is not a predictable system, but the result of a long history of trying to find a common way to communicate across cultures, we make it clear to them that to be good readers they need to be figuring out what makes sense the whole time they are reading. We free them from being rule appliers, from being mechanical, and from waiting to understand. Just as when they learned to speak, they can always make some sense from text. We are born "little scientists," naturally hypothesizing about what we hear, see and touch, literally all the time. In a culture of literacy, children are constantly reminded that they can "figure it out!"

## Encourage Students to Start Stories

"Whoa, wait a minute," you are probably saying to yourself. You probably deal with "he said, she said" all the time. Exactly the point! Left to their own devices, children will tell stories about their experiences of conflict and hurt feelings. But you can take advantage of this propensity to tell stories by encouraging it. Students are trying to understand their experience through stories. Miguel Sabido pioneered Mexican telenovas, soap operas with social messages in the 1970s. When characters in his "stories" suffered because of not being able to read, and then got help, the number of people signing up for literacy instruction soared, more than 800,000 adults enrolled in education classes. When family planning issues were addressed over a period of 10 years, population growth dropped by 34%. The telenovela stories let people hear, retell, and take to heart stories on current social issues.

Listen to stories of conflict, helplessness, and jealousy you hear from students, and ask students to change the names and to write about them. The story-writing contest one month can be on a social topic that is immediate and relevant. Students can write to topics on your list, collected from school issues, or identify others in their lives. Specify that the stories must be fiction, so names and events are changed, but the story is nevertheless about an experience that is familiar and local in importance. Ask that the story show how the characters learn to make things better and are successful in improving the situation, their feelings, and their relationships. They can even write multiple endings based on the decisions their characters made. Like Shakespeare and Sabido your students will begin to write tales on universal issues, change how they think about current challenges in their lives, and see writing and reading as tools for change.

Models for stories of this kind are classic fairy tales and fables as well as stories of children learning to work out their issues with each other without adult intervention such: *Talk And Work It Out*, by Cheri J. Meiners and

Meredith Johnson, *Stick Up for Yourself: Every Kid's Guide to Personal Power & Positive Self-Esteem,* by Gershen Kaufman, Lev Raphael, Pamela Espeland, and by Gregory Stock, *Don't Laugh at Me,* by Steve Seskin, Allen Shamblin, Glin Dibley, and *What Do You Stand For? For Kids: A Guide To Building Character,* by Barbara A. Lewis, Marjorie Lisovskis.

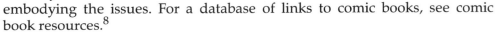

For more on how traditional fairy tales teach basic values and problem solving, see Bruno Bettleheim's classic book, *The Uses of Enchantment: The Meaning and Importance of Fairy Tales.* For a different take on the classic fairy tales, see books like: *The True Story of the 3 Little Pigs,* by Jon Scieszka; Eugene Trivizas's *The Three Little Wolves and the Big Bad Pig;* Marilyn Tolhurst's *Somebody and The Three Blairs;* and Betty Fraser's Fractured Fairy Tales.[7]

Comic books are also great models of morality tales with heroes and villains embodying the issues. For a database of links to comic books, see comic book resources.[8]

What can your students write about? Some issues are developmental while others seem to cross grade levels because they are classic struggles over property, position or attention. Phrased in student language, some "hot" topics would include:

| *Social Issue Topics for Elementary Student Writing* |
|---|
| ◆ Disrespect: S/he wasn't nice to me or s/he said … about me |
| ◆ Isolation: I felt left out when … or I wanted to be included when … |
| ◆ Disloyalty: S/he told my secret |
| ◆ Friendship: S/he isn't my friend anymore or I want to be her friend |
| ◆ Power: S/he or they won't do what I want/say |
| ◆ Fear: I was afraid to … s/he hit me … |
| ◆ Deceit: S/he lied to me or s/he went behind my back |
| ◆ Theft: S/he took my stuff |

7. http://www.acs.ucalgary.ca/~dkbrown/fft.html
8. http://www.comicbookresources.com/resources/links/

Whatever the issues in your school, encourage all grade levels to participate. Small children can dictate to their teachers what should be done when someone hits you, or takes your things. These responses are often as funny as they are insightful as they are "out of the mouths of babes." Notice how these parallel the seven basic plots!

## Post Story Ideas

"In the beginning …" "Once upon a time …" and "My mama told me … Each of these phrases carries a special meaning or tradition. They signal time and place, reality, or imagination, and hint at what will come in the story. Post these in the halls, the classrooms, and the libraries. Use them as collection places for other story starters, for the names of stories that begin that way, and for original stories. You are unlocking the door of story beginnings by helping students see the patterns in beginnings and where they lead. Emphasize the strategies behind the beginnings so students see the options. For example:

| Story beginnings | What they may signal |
|---|---|
| In the beginning … | A story told over time to show changes or help the reader understand why things are they way they are now |
| Once upon a time … | A timeless story, often a fairy tale or other exaggerated story where the background is given in the beginning |
| My mama told me … | A story about a lesson learned or ignored |
| It just so happened that … | A story you enter in the middle of what is happening |
| We were talking … | A story told through the characters and their experience |
| We never noticed before, but … You wouldn't believe it now, but … | A story that begins with the climax or big event, and then fills in how it all happened |
| When we look back on the year 2007 … | A story told from the future looking back on now |

| To understand what happened you need to hear from John, Jaime, and Litka (or other characters) | A story that builds through the separate pieces told by individual characters |
|---|---|

Make beginnings the theme for the opening of school. In the first week, have every class post their favorite beginnings in the hall. The next week, each class can add examples of stories with those beginnings. In the next week, they can add a conversation bubble saying what each beginning signals, and the last week they can add stories written by the class using those beginnings or others they add to the display. The idea is to have many discussions about beginnings throughout the school so children see the variety of beginnings that are available to them and to create conversations about beginnings among students and faculty. Follow the emphasis on beginnings with a focus on middles and ends later in the year. See the sample calendars for exploring middles in November and endings in April. Use the same four-week process to build from an awareness of the variety of strategies for beginnings, middles, and ends, to collecting samples from literature, to analyzing those examples to define the different strategies in conversation bubbles to using them in original writing. Moving from awareness to metacognition through analysis and application helps students consolidate their understanding of the options and how they work.

## Summary

This chapter has discussed language as both simple and complex. Language is simple because it has elements that children understand through their lives and oral language. It is complex because the rules for pronunciation and spelling apply only some of the time. Children use all the structures of language in their oral language so they can learn to use cues to develop their understanding of written language and how it connects to oral language. Since children are hardwired for figuring things out, talking about written language as a puzzle to make sense of empowers them to learn all the nuances of the English language. On the flip side, students have dramatic stories to tell that bring intensity and meaning to their writing, causing them to explore different structures to say what they want to say.

## Reflection

Take a moment to reflect on your school's culture. Are reading and writing talked about as hard and time-consuming, or as interesting and challenging? Do children write stories about the drama in their lives or only what they did last weekend? Do teachers and families know the types of sentences, paragraphs, and plots? Are they posted in classrooms with examples? Do children experiment with different language structures and discuss the results?

# Chapter 16

# What Does it Mean to Be Literate?

### Questions to Ponder Before Reading

♦ What do you notice about students who pick up reading and writing easily?

♦ How do you get children to learn and use new strategies for reading and writing?

♦ When and how do you ask children to reflect on what makes them successful in reading and writing?

Everyone in the school community needs to believe that he or she can find a way to help each child to learn to read at grade level. Belinda Williams[1] tells of her experience with working with teachers in schools with differences between minority and majority student achievement. In schools with no gap, teachers believed it was their responsibility to find a way for each and every student to learn. In schools with large achievement gaps, teachers said they believed all children could learn, but when pressed said they were doing all they could and it was up to the students to learn—a very different perspective!

Regardless of race, ethnicity, gender, or socioeconomic status, every child can be reached some way, some how by someone in the school community. It's a matter of perseverance, careful observation, and diagnosis, having a large repertoire of strategies to model and teach, and keeping the students' interest and confidence high with honest, helpful feedback.

Literate students are strategic, able to reflect, confident, ready to learn, and develop knowledge through reading and writing. Each of these behav-

---

1. Williams, B. (Ed.). (1996). *Closing the achievement gap: A vision for changing beliefs and practices.* Alexandria, VA: ASCD.

iors enhances the others. For example, when students are ready to learn, they feel confident in learning situations. When they are able to reflect, they track their progress, and tend to attribute it to their own efforts in using the strategies, which in turn build their confidence.

## Literate Students Are Strategic

Focusing on strategies is the key to helping students feel confident and motivated enough to pay attention to instruction. When Donald Schunk[2] focused students on learning goals rather than outcome goals, they learned more and were more satisfied with their learning. This seems to be true regardless of whether students are learning fractions, how to write a paragraph or how to throw darts.[3]

## Literate Students Are Ready to Learn

Students are ready to learn when they ask a question, when they have a need, or when they care about the results. Skillful teachers use diagnosis to identify where students are and give them work that is challenging without being frustrating, and worthwhile in the students' eyes. This is the optimal learning condition. Using different size groups and having one-on-one time with students gives the teacher the information she needs to offer those "just right" books and instruction, model expert strategies, and let students see each other as models that have them pushing to learn more.

## Literate Students Are Able to Reflect

When students are expected to reflect on what and how they are learning, they develop the skills of self-regulation. They get used to feedback, begin to value it, and use it to self-correct. People do this naturally in areas where they

2. Schunk, D. H., & Pajares, F. (2002). The development of academic self-efficacy. In A. Wigfield & J. Eccles (Eds.), *Development of achievement motivation* (pp. 16-32). San Diego, CA: Academic Press.
3. Zimmerman, B. J., & Kitsantas. A. (1996). Self-regulated learning of a motoric skill: The role of goal-setting and self-monitoring. *Journal of Applied Sport Psychology, 18,* 60-67.

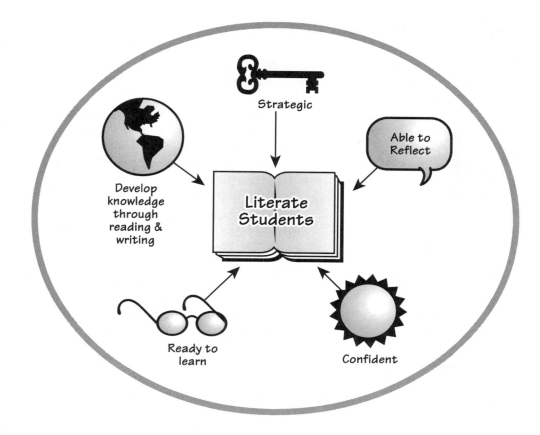

want to learn, but school situations do not always do a good job of supporting this aspect of learning.

Ask teachers to have students spend at least 10% of their instructional time on having students reflect on what and how they learning. Model this in your faculty meetings and when you visit classrooms.

Work with a team of teachers to set up systems for paper or digital portfolios to show student progress over time. Integrate portfolios into parent conferences so teachers and parents can discuss children's progress based on artifacts of their work.

When you talk with students, ask them to tell you what and how they are learning. Then ask if you can tell their learning story to others. Write it up, pass it on, tell it to the whole class right then, or in some other way show you understand the importance of reflection.

Think out aloud. When you make announcements about decision, talk about how the decision was made. Let students know that reflection is a big part of life and learning.

# Literate Students Are Confident

Children are naturally confident until they repeatedly fail and don't know why. When they don't feel in control of their successes and failures, they lose  the confidence to go on learning. They don't know what to focus on and how to improve. Teachers and parents build students' confidence by making it clear that the use of strategies is the key to success. Then, with regular feedback during practice, and time for the student to reflect, the child and adult talk about their progress (or lack of it) in terms of how well they are using the strategies. This connection is crucial.

The message is always that you can learn the strategy and that you will make progress, and if you don't, it is because you need to use the strategy more effectively. Through feedback and reflection, students learn that success and failure are part of learning, and that progress is always possible. They are not stupid or hopeless or inadequate. Their natural self-confidence is sustained when they have a clear understanding of the learning goals, see the strategies modeled, and get honest immediate feedback on their progress that connects back to their use of the strategies.

When you praise students, be specific in connecting success with use of strategies.

When you talk with teachers about students, ask what strategies the students use successfully.

When you talk with parents, emphasize the strategies their child, or children of their age, are learning to use successfully. Pull out a book, model a strategy for them, and encourage them to talk with their child about using it. Remind them that learning to use any strategy takes time and practice so they need to be patient rather than impatient with progress. We don't learn to use strategies simply by having someone tell us we need to.

# Literate Students Develop Knowledge and Skills Through Reading and Writing

The most motivating factor for students to read is to learn things they want to learn. The most motivating factor for students to write is to communicate something they care about to an important audience. Frank Smith,[4] an important thinker about literacy and learning in the last half century, once said that it was useless to correct a student's writing unless he or she asked you to. He had observed that unless a student cared about the quality of the writing, cared about the audience, or cared about learning, any feedback would fall on deaf ears. He suggested that the question for teachers was not, "How do I get them to write better?" but "How do I get them to ask for feedback to care about their writing?"

Make reading and writing about learning, not about skill development. Remember the lunchtime sharing idea to showcase student interests by having talent talks during lunch to emphasize reading to learn. Show your support of student writers by putting copies of student-authored books on display everywhere other students can pick them up and read them. Have teach-ins where upper-grade students teach what they are learning in social studies to younger students, or local clubs as travelogues, or at community nights. Create a speaker's bureau with your students who become experts on different topics. Get their writing published in local papers or published in school newsletters. Create and celebrate expertise and reading and writing skill will.

## Teacher Favorites

Survey the faculty for their favorite children's books and stories. At a faculty meeting, have them share their favorites, tell the story of what the books mean to them, and how they share, or would like to share that book with their classes. Feature a book each week with a recommendation from a teacher. Place the book in the office with the teacher's recommendation. Have the teacher do a review of the book in a morning announcement. Give away a copy of the book. Put a picture of the book and the teacher's recommendation in the weekly packet of announcements that go home to families. Create a notebook of recommendations for each grade level with room for students to add their own recommendations when they read the books. If you have a

4. Smith, F. (2003). *Unspeakable acts, unnatural practices: Flaws and fallacies in scientific reading instruction*. Portsmouth, NH: Heinemann.

school Web site, have an electronic version of these recommendations. Look to online booksellers for examples of, "What other readers have said about this book."

## Student Favorites

In each class, ask teachers to ask students to list their top three books for all time and their favorite books for the year. Meeting by grade level, teachers can compile a top-10 list for their grade-level students, and ask students who chose those books to write recommendations. These can be shared in the same way as the teacher list, or consider having a top 10 each month, like the *New York Times* bestseller list for fiction and nonfiction, posted in the library with copies of the books. People share their ideas about books in a culture of literacy. They talk about books, write about books and above all read and write a lot!

## Summary

This chapter has been about creating and modeling high expectations for teaching and learning strategies, for students to know about themselves through reflection, for beginning where you are, for providing and accepting honest feedback, for building up confidence, and for creating and celebrating expertise. Do any one of these and it will feed the others. Set the expectations, model in your every move, and celebrate out loud when you see it happening.

## Reflection

Take a moment to make notes about ideas from this chapter in the plan book in Section II? What messages does your school's culture send about how ready your students are to learn, how strategic they are, and how confident they should be?: How does your school's culture encourage learning *through* reading and writing? How often and in what ways do you ask students to reflect on what they know about language?

# Chapter 17

# How Does a Culture of Literacy Develop Among Teachers in a School?

### Questions to Ponder Before Reading

♦ What in your school's culture supports teachers working together? What gets in the way?

♦ Does your faculty share a vision of how literacy develops? What do you believe?

♦ How do you use data to understand what your students can do?

2 + 2 really does equal 5. We are more effective together than we are apart. A few leaders in a school can make a lot of changes and implement new ideas and strategies, but without involving the whole faculty, some people will feel left out and eventually start to resist or undermine your whole school activities. You need everyone to feel and BE part of the solution, or they will be part of the problem. Get started on the right foot by building a vision together of how children become literate that can underpin all your efforts. In this chapter, you will read about how reading skills develop and how your faculty can use this knowledge to understand what children can do, and how to nudge them forward. When teachers understand what there is to know it helps enormously in listening to children to see what they are able to do well.

## Build a Vision Together

What do you believe children are capable of at different ages and stages? How do children become literate? How do you decide what to teach when?

What do they need to know and believe about language? How much time will they get on their own? How do you teach writing? Should children all read the same book? Use the same story map? How should we ask children to respond to nonfiction texts—dialog journals, by answering questions, by asking questions?

If you believe that children are resilient and soak up new experience, you immerse them in opportunities and watch what they latch on to. If you believe they are limited by their prior experience, you may not push them to go beyond what they can do at first. If you believe worksheets are good practice, children in your classroom will spend less time reading and talking about what they read. If you believe children need to spell correctly and use proper punctuation whenever they write, you will spend more time teaching that and correcting their papers rather than getting them to read more and write more for real audiences so they care about using standard English.

To find out what your colleagues believe about these issues and more, begin to shift discussions away from logistics and toward philosophy. Be patient in developing these conversations since this may be unfamiliar territory. Start with asking everyone to react to statements. Ask teachers to share classroom practices related to their beliefs. Accept everyone's ideas by posting them and acknowledging differences.

The idea is to build openness and respect so the faculty can have honest discussions about how children become literate—not about their teaching, but about learning. This honest dialog allows people to consider what they know and don't know rather than feeling uninformed or isolated, or operating out of unexamined beliefs or misinformation. Everyone has something to contribute from their experience as learners and their observations of how their students learn. Just as with students in the classroom, Vygotsky's concept of the zone of proximal development is at work here. By listening closely to each other in an understanding mode, rather than a critical one, the faculty will learn from each other and will be better able to reflect on their practice. The discussion will create momentum for change.

Consider one of these statements to begin your discussions. Notice the beliefs in your school and use them for discussion. Map the responses on a continuum from strongly agree to strongly disagree. Then add examples of different viewpoints.

- Worksheets in reading are good practice.
- Students learn to write by reading stories first, then reading nonfiction to learn later, around fourth grade.
- Teaching comprehension strategies has to wait until students are good at decoding.
- Students are not interested in nonfiction as much as fiction.
- Invented spelling and punctuation lets students develop bad habits.
- Students learn to read better by reading more.

Post the results of your discussion in the faculty room and refer to it in your individual discussions with teachers, helping them to extend their understanding and examine their beliefs about how children become literate. In subsequent faculty meetings, introduce research, share stories, and invite examples from students in your school that support an in-depth understanding of the milestones in literacy development. Discuss the evidence, what you all see in children, and the underlying beliefs that these challenge.

In this chapter you will see one way of portraying the continuum. Some faculties prefer lists of skills, behaviors and attitudes, others prefer paragraph descriptions that correspond with leveled texts. You may use several ways to portray the development. The form of the developmental continuum is less important than what it conveys—a shared vision of how children become literate—and the belief behind it—that children DO become more literate at different paces and that specific instruction based on what they are able to do, matters a great deal in how they develop.

## Use Data to Open Up Discussions

Using data is a terrific way to open up discussions about how children are developing. How are students doing in specific areas? How many are making progress? In what areas? Where can we see that our instruction is making a difference?

The best measure is the child's progress against him or herself. Ongoing assessments of how children are understanding words, sentences, and texts keeps everyone focused on helping children to make progress. When you add discussions, the specific strengths, needs of children, and what is helping them, everyone strengthens their understanding of the process of students becoming literate and learns about what works to help them develop.

In grade-level teams, plan to discuss at least one student a week. Have each teacher on the team bring samples of a couple of students' work. What is the child reading? What are her current interests? What does she under-

stand about written language? What does
she struggle to understand? Having discussions about the strategies to use with
individual children based on data about
them is a great way to learn from each
other. It brings the developmental continuum in reading and writing to life so the
patterns in individual children's performance are more readily apparent.

Use what you learn in grade-level
teams to create an overall developmental
continuum. Whether you use the first approach of having discussions about
beliefs and understandings, or the second, of using data to develop the continuum, what is important is to make it a working document that informs
everyone teaching and learning.

## Understanding Literacy Development

Theories and research about how people learn to read fills volumes due to
several factors: the complexity of the relationship of oral and written language, individual differences in people and their backgrounds, and the
systemic nature of the purposes, mechanics, and components of reading and
writing. Becoming literate is systemic in that the purposes, components, and
mechanics inform and contribute to each other. For example, when a student
wants to write letters (emails) successfully, that purpose leads her to attend to
the structure of personal communication, to learn greetings and closings, and
to use rhetorical structures such as questions, to increase the likelihood the
person will write back, which will generate more emails. Or when a student
is consistently able to "sound out" (use phonological decoding) words to pronounce them correctly, she is more likely to understand the meaning of the
word in the context of the sentence or paragraph, which in turns makes her
more eager to sound out words successfully.

It is critical to understand and use this systemic relationship of students'
developing understanding of letter-sound relationships, the structure of
words and sentences and the strategies to comprehend written texts in the
teaching and learning process. When you realize that these understandings
develop simultaneously, and at different rates in different children, you
become focused on watching and listening to what children are doing with
language. For example, invented spelling represents a breakthrough in children's understanding of how language works because they are using letters
to represent sounds and meaning, if only on a limited and inaccurate basis. In

the act of inventing spelling, children are telling us they understand that letters are different from one another, that they represent what we say, and that they carry meaning. From invented spelling children don't spell worse; they only spell better, adding more and more sounds that accurately represent the sounds they hear in the words they want to use. When they "read" their stories written with these invented spellings of words, they show us what they intend others to comprehend what they have written.

What follows is an overview of literacy development in terms of the basic elements of printed language. This overview is a place for you to start with your faculty in discussing what you know from experience and the research. Some may find it too detailed, while others may wish for more detail. It is not meant to be exclusive or exhaustive. What is important is that your faculty develops a shared understanding of the facets of literacy development. It is not linear since children are learning on multiple fronts and in fits and starts. As a reference for going deeper into the research on literacy development, the National Research Council book, *Preventing Reading Difficulties in Young Children*,[1] does an excellent job of reviewing the research on literacy development and what is essential for instruction to support development.

## Letters

Since English is based on an alphabet, rather than characters such as Chinese, children must understand what is called the alphabetic principle: that print represents the sounds of language from individual phonemes to indivisible sound entities called syllables, to blended or combined phonemes in words, to words strung together in sentences.

Phonological awareness is recognizing the correspondence of letters (graphemes) and sounds (phonemes) of language. Phonemic awareness is the component of phonological awareness that focuses on the sounds. Children first isolate sounds in spoken words, such as "f" in "fall," then blend sounds such as "pl" and "play." This is generally followed by adding, subtracting, and rearranging sounds in words to make different words in playing with rhyming words, words that begin the same (alliteration) and nonsense words. Eventually children recognize that every word is a sequence of sounds. Phonemic awareness is closely related to speech perception, that is, the ability to detect sounds of the language and discriminate between similar words such as "tell" and "fell." While phonemic awareness often develops in

---

1. Snow, C. E., Burns, S., & Griffin, P. (Eds.). (1998). *Preventing reading difficulties in young children*. Washington, DC: National Academy Press.

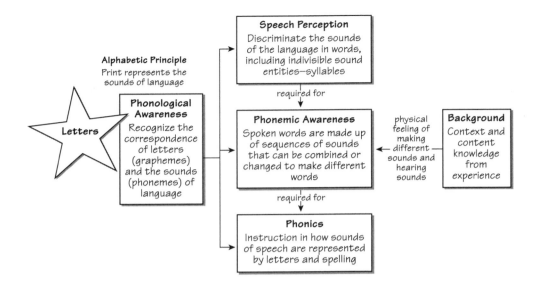

preschool, when children do not come from literacy rich backgrounds where they were read to, talked to, and listened to, they may benefit from phonics instruction that shows them how the sounds of speech are represented by letters and spellings, but only in context, where they are using letter or sound cues to recognize a word that makes sense.

Explicit instruction of the phonological structure of oral language and the connections between phonemes (sounds) and spellings is important to direct children's attention to the role of the alphabet.

Being clear with children about "looking" at letters and "listening" for sounds helps them learn how each of these systems helps them recognize a word that makes sense in the context of the sentence, paragraph or story. Knowing that children will most likely focus on the beginning and endings before the middles of words lets the teacher know to praise their instant recognition, and help them to focus on the other parts of the words.

## Words

Reading begins when children begin to map the letters and spellings of words onto sounds and speech units. Confidence grows when they are in on this secret about language: *What is said can be written down and it doesn't change each time you read it. You just have to persevere in looking at all the letters and using what you know to figure out how to say the word and relate it to the words you have heard.* Word identification and comprehension are reciprocal processes supporting each other as students gain proficiency in each. Children's vocabularies grow exponentially with experience, and then lift off as they develop automaticity in word recognition and comprehension, thinking of the words in context, using sound cues instead of letter cues in a recursive process that usually happens quickly in the search for meaning.

Word identification is being able to pronounce words. In the beginning children recognize words more as images than letters with shapes. As they gain recognition of a sound in a word, that sound *is* the word. Finally, they recognize beginning sounds and associate them with a word. Ending and medial sound recognition follow. Finally, students attend to all the letters in a word to "decode" it. This use of all the sounds to identify a word is called "phonological decoding." Learning the spelling and pronunciation of words supports this decoding, and is supported by it, as does learning the structure or "morphology" of words, the roots, prefixes, and suffixes. But skilled read-

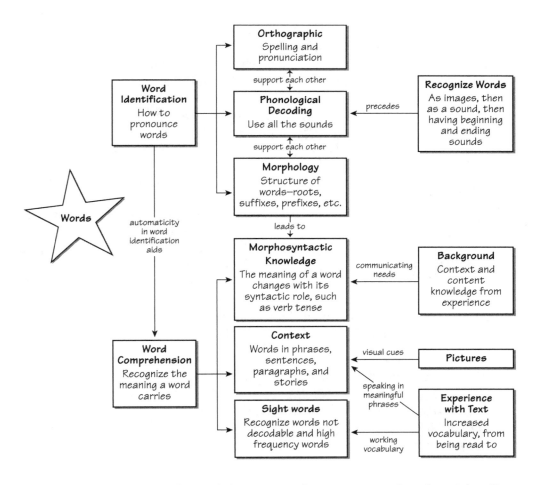

ers don't decode very often or very thoroughly since they can usually figure out what the word means from a few of its characteristics. Good readers know it trips you up when you slow down too much since you risk losing track of what is going on. They substitute "blank" or "blah" for unknown words to keep reading until it makes sense, or reread to see what might make sense based on some part of the word that is familiar.

Word comprehension is defined as understanding the meaning a word carries from recognizing it, from personal experience, prior reading experience, and from context. Students first comprehend words that they decode and connect with their oral understanding of the word. Very quickly, they learn to use pictures, the sentence in which they find the word, and the overall text structure to make sense of words they can decode but are not necessarily familiar with from their lived or read experience. The context of the sentence, paragraph, and story provide clues to the meaning of a word. Later, students use the role of words in sentences to understand their meaning. This "morphosyntactic" knowledge lets them distinguish different meanings in words that have similar sounds, such as "have flown" versus "fly" and "flow" based on the role of the word in the sentence. Word comprehension is knowing the difference between a house and a horse because it's important to know whether you are living in a horse or riding a house.

Eventually all these tools merge and students are in a kind of "meaning stream" that lets them figure out words from beginning and ending sounds and "seeing" the word as a whole. Consider the following:

*Cna yuo raed tihs? Of cosure yuo cna. Yuo cna aulaclty uesdnatnrd waht yuo aer rdanieg if the frist and lsat ltteer are in the rghit pclae. It deosn't mttaer in waht oredr the ltteers in a wrod are sncie the mnid is phaonmneal at srceahnig for maennig. The pweor of the hmuan mind is raednig wlohe wrods not ivindidaul lteters.*

# Sentences

As children are developing an understanding of the written word, they are simultaneously noticing more and more about how words work. Words hardly ever appear alone, except for words like "yes" or "no" or "wow." Just as children first say individual words, they are often attracted to words that are fun to say, or that have personal importance to them, such as their name or a word that captures something they want to write about.

But most of the time, words appear in groups just as they do in conversation. By kindergarten, most children are using complete sentences to describe who is doing what, when, and why in their speech. "He pushed me down on the sidewalk just now and I hurt my knee." They are well aware of actors and actions, of time, and location and even consequences. They capture all this in their spoken language. They have heard similar scenarios in stories, and they are adept at asking questions and making excuses. "If he hadn't pushed me down, I wouldn't have hurt my knee and we would still be friends."

Children know about the different types of sentences: declarative, interrogatory, exclamatory, and imperative, and they use them in speaking. To support reading and writing sentences, instruction needs to call students' attention to the punctuation that identifies each type of sentence as having different emotions. Students learn that sentences carry meaning through punctuation by capturing the intonation through "! . ?" Just as students learn to attend to how sounds are represented by letters, they also begin to attend to this punctuation and the structure of sentences as representations of the way we speak. Teaching punctuation as a way to capture the intonation behind intention can be intriguing to students as they repeat a single sentence with different ending punctuation.

This growing syntactic knowledge allows students to use the structure of sentences to understand the meaning of words, phrases, and whole sentences. By school age, children are already using difficult sentence structures in speech to communicate about immediate experience and ideas such as "What if?" and "It reminds me of …" They speak in phrases if asked to slow down indicating they understand that phrases carry more meaning than individual words. This leads to phrase reading in which they read meaningful chunks aloud and silently. Instruction needs to call attention to these meaningful parts of sentences. Students first understand nouns, then verbs, then modifiers, and finally function words like articles, conjunctions, and prepositions.

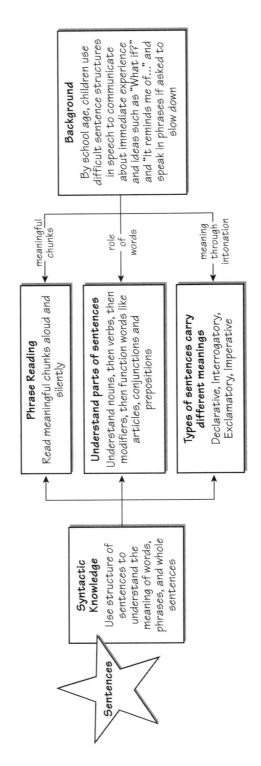

**Background**

By school age, children use difficult sentence structures in speech to communicate about immediate experience and ideas such as "What if?" and "It reminds me of..." and speak in phrases if asked to slow down

meaningful chunks

role of words

meaning through intonation

**Phrase Reading**

Read meaningful chunks aloud and silently

**Understand parts of sentences**

Understand nouns, then verbs, then modifiers, then function words like articles, conjunctions and prepositions

**Types of sentences carry different meanings**

Declarative, Interrogatory, Exclamatory, Imperative

**Syntactic Knowledge**

Use structure of sentences to understand the meaning of words, phrases, and whole sentences

**Sentences**

Again, skills and strategies merge in the service of making meaning. The order of the words in a sentence is less important than the overall meaning derived by the reader. Reading between the lines is as natural as filling in words when listening to someone in a loud place or in a bad telephone connection. No one has trouble understanding Yoda of Star Wars fame, even though his sentences do not use standard syntax.

*Found me you have. Here for my help, you are, yes? Find what you are looking for, you will. I will help you not. Go there I cannot. Know what I am talking about, do you?*[2]

The brain puts the pieces back together in ways that make sense, whether they are letters in a word or words in a sentence. This wonderful function is a survival tool at the most basic level and confirms that comprehension is the key—everything comes back to the reader thinking about what makes sense.

## Paragraphs

Just as sentences gather up words and phrases into units of meaning, so do paragraphs take an idea and make a point about it, visually grouping sentences around a main idea, adding description and extending understanding through elaboration and summarizing. Children go from seeing a page with a few sentences to an indented or separated group of sentences that signal the reader to expect a single idea. They begin to notice that they have to pay closer attention to longer paragraphs with more complexity or detail. They come to expect that shorter paragraphs often build on each other to paint a larger picture. They begin to expect each paragraph to stand alone, using the structure and purpose of paragraphs as tools for meaning.

Children bring a background of understanding people's intentions from their body language and intonation. They are used to routines that focus on a single function or idea, like going to lunch, or "silent reading" time. These focused situations are analogs for paragraphs that carry a chunk of meaning. Children understand that form and purpose are linked in communication, and that paragraphs are the structure that communicates about a single idea. This understanding provides helpful background for understanding the different purposes of paragraphs: narration, exposition, definition, classification, description, process analysis, and persuasion.

2. For more on Yodish, see http://www.yodajeff.com/pages/talk/

**Background**
Children understand people's intentions and how they communicate them from oral language and social experience

key ideas

purposes

**Paragraphs are a visual grouping of a unit of meaning**
Conveying a single idea, topic, or speaker that can stand alone

**Paragraphs have different purposes**
Narration, Exposition, Definition, Classification, Description, Process, Analysis, Persuasion

**Purpose and Structure**
Use structure and purpose to comprehend

**Paragraphs**

# Texts: Fiction and Nonfiction

In life, stories unfold and are told in familiar ways. In a similar way, information is communicated in recognizable patterns. At the same time children are learning how words, sentences, and paragraphs have structures that carry meaning, they are hearing, telling, and living stories. They are getting information from different people under different conditions for different reasons. By preschool, they can distinguish between "pretend" and "real" stories. By first grade they are reading nonfiction to learn and reading fiction for enjoyment and to understand their own experience.

Just as paragraphs have different purposes, stories have those seven basic plots: overcoming the monster, rags to riches, questing, voyage and return, comedy, tragedy, and rebirth. Knowing these structures helps students to make connections between stories, see through to basic purposes, and recognize the stories they write about their own lives.

Students are reading to learn from the time they are very little. Like adults, they develop interests that can be pursued through reading. Whether it's dinosaurs or baseball, trucks or princesses, nonfiction books feed children's interests. They may read to find out how to do something, such as bake a cake, or build a model. They may read to compare or to find out answers. Again, the structure carries important information so letting students in on some basic organizations of nonfiction texts focuses their attention on the structure as well as the content. This enhances their comprehension and prepares them to use these structures in their own writing. Some basic organizations of nonfiction text are: descriptive, problem and solution, time sequence or order, compare and contrast, cause and effect, and question and answer.

Developmentally, students understand the purpose and structure of descriptive writing early on. While not initially adept at writing time sequence or order, by second grade they are keen to try to write "good directions." They learn problem and solution through autobiographies and biographies, and can generalize from fiction in which characters solve problems in their lives. Most students can recognize and use the compare and contrast organization about immediate, concrete objects or experience in kindergarten. They have experience comparing cookies, toys, movies, and games to make choices. Children's "opinions" about what they like and dislike and their reasons form a strong foundation for compare/contrast text comprehension. Cause and effect is also dependent on maturation. Causation is as familiar to the toddler chasing birds in the park as it is to the preschooler who gets a "time out" for being disrespectful. Connecting this core knowledge of cause and effect to text happens early on in fairy tales and just needs to be walked over to nonfiction texts that explain why birds can fly and how fire-

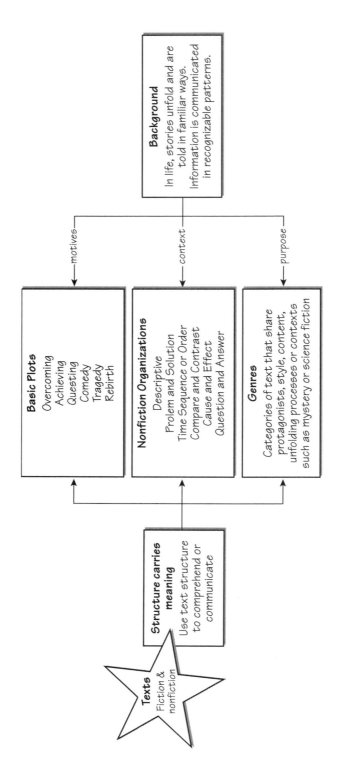

**Background**
In life, stories unfold and are told in familiar ways. Information is communicated in recognizable patterns.

motives

context

purpose

**Basic Plots**
Overcoming
Achieving
Questing
Comedy
Tragedy
Rebirth

**Nonfiction Organizations**
Descriptive
Prolem and Solution
Time Sequence or Order
Compare and Contrast
Cause and Effect
Question and Answer

**Genres**
Categories of text that share protagonists, style, content, unfolding processes or contexts such as mystery or science fiction

**Structure carries meaning**
Use text structure to comprehend or communicate

**Texts**
Fiction & nonfiction

fighters put out fires. Since the majority of reading adults do is nonfiction, whether in printed or electronic text, students need to be prepared to read effectively for information.

Another set of structural clues comes from the concept of genres, whole categories of texts that share protagonists, style, content, unfolding processes, or contexts such as mystery or science fiction. Like knowing how to read the features of a landscape through layers of information about topography, temperature, plant growth, moisture, population, and elevation, knowing about genres lets students comprehend texts at yet another level. A short list of genres could include: biography/autobiography, fantasy, historical fiction, myths and legends, poetry, science fiction, fairy tales, folktales, mystery, nonfiction, realistic fiction, and short stories.

## Make the Continuum a Living, Working Tool

Throughout the development described in the sections above, children are generally as engaged as we are in discovering the patterns and nuances of language. Unless they are burned out from too much failure or correction, they are naturally inclined to active processing of ideas and information. When they want to know something, are hooked on a story, need information to buy something, or go somewhere, they will tackle the most difficult texts and even ask for help if they feel like they aren't "getting it."

In the late seventies, I was in a masters degree program in reading at State University of New York at Brockport. Professor Roberta Fullagher and others had founded the program the year before and were very excited to focus on the emerging field of reading. We studied Chomsky to understand how sentences were constructed and deconstructed. We learned to listen very carefully to children reading and do running records to uncover how they thought about language. We studied children's books and even wrote our own. The goal was to tune our ears to where children were in a developmental continuum of understanding written language. They wanted us to be able to sit with a child and uncover what they understood about how language works, so we would know how to affirm for them

> *Focusing on the continuum also makes it clear that reading and writing are the crucible for learning more.*

what was working in their quests for meaning, and to offer them more effective strategies than those they were using that led to the pattern of errors we observed. Yes, we learned many diagnostic tools and interventions, but the goal was for us to internalize a developmental continuum.

An important goal of faculty discussions is to have everyone internalize the continuum, so they can see children where they are, and move them forward. Having this as the goal solves a lot of problems—like seeing children as IN the process of learning rather than deficient, like how knowing what will move children forward, rather than having to find activities to fill time, and like knowing what to teach them next instead of marching through a curriculum. Knowing the continuum also makes it clear that instruction and experience are what move children ahead—not worksheets or practice. Practice may consolidate learning, but it is the conversation with children about their strategies—how those strategies are working for them, and what else to try—that gives them new ways to think about language and to replace less efficient strategies. Focusing on the continuum also makes it clear that reading and writing are the crucible for learning more. Wanting to know what will happen next, having the support of structure to make meaning, and wanting to write about one's own experience propel students forward in using language well. Making and communicating meaning are real, rewarding, and get results.

As the faculty uses the continuum to understand how student literacy develops, the continuum will reflect the evolving understanding of the faculty. As a living document, it can reflect the nuances teachers observe in their students. As teachers use the continuum, have them capture ideas, strategies and methods for observing students and interacting with them to help them develop new strategies. They can identify students that exemplify the different understandings on the continuum and tell their stories. You can create a resource file in the faculty room, reading resource room, or electronic space where ideas and resources can be posted and used.

## Share the Continuum With Students and Their Families

Use the continuum with students and families. Clear goals are critical for everyone to be moving in the same direction. To make the goals concrete, consider recreating report cards, interim reports, and parent conferences around the continuum. In a review of the literature, Marzano (2006)[3] found that students increased their achievement when the feedback they received was specific and immediate. When the language of the goals and the routines for feedback are consistent, students and teachers develop a culture based on a

---

3. Marzano, R. (2006). *Classroom assessment and grading that works.* Alexandria, VA: ASCD.

success orientation. The continuum sends this message that it is okay to be "on the way to getting better."

Using the continuum, you can create individual profiles for students. Like Individual Educational Plans (IEP), the continuum can be used to identify both the strengths and needs of a student and plan for them. I used a developmental continuum to conference with my sixth-grade students, so we could celebrate each new understanding and discuss what they would be doing next. By charting students' learning progress, they were more motivated to learn. The information about how they were doing, what they had already learned to do and what their next set of goals were, enabled them to feel successful. This added level of metacognition became a natural part of the learning process so they understood why they were successful and what they needed to do next to continue to become better readers and writers.

To take the idea of a profile based on a developmental continuum one step further consider portfolios. This electronic or paper-based tool can help connect student work to the skills and strategies in the continuum. In some schools, classes have folders labeled by the larger categories of skills and strategies where they place their writing and reflections. Then for conferences with teachers or parents, each student collects all his or her work from the folders and reflects on progress to create a portfolio of work representing personal growth. Other schools have electronic portfolios in which students reflect in short video or audio clips and collect evidence for proficiency in the skills and strategies. In a project in New London, Connecticut, we found the use of video recordings to be particularly motivating to students because the idea of an audience for their reflections was very immediate. When they reviewed their video recordings, they were their own audience along with the teacher and perhaps a few classmates in their collaborative group. Within a few weeks, students became very articulate in talking about their reading and writing. LeTicia talked about her story as "pretty good but needing more details." Jime said he thought talking about his story helped him to "make it better for people to read." Jazmine reflected at the end of the first marking period, "my best writing is when I write about my friends because I know a lot about them."

Regardless of how you connect student work to the continuum of reading and writing, you will want to include examples of students' words, behaviors and interactions about what they understand about language. Using the continuum with students and their families creates a culture in which conversation about progress is comfortable and helpful, and success is based on effort.

## Summary

This chapter has explored three key ideas for developing a culture of literacy among faculty: (1) building a vision together; (2) using data for decision making, and; (3) developing and using a developmental continuum for reading and writing. Since a culture, by definition, is ever-evolving, reflecting the people within it and their goals, the conversations you have, the routines you develop, and the tools you use should all be explicitly focused on your goals. With that focus, the question is always, "How does _____ support our culture of literacy?"

## Reflection

Does your faculty share a vision of how students become literate? How can you build conversation about literacy development into your time together? What do your students understand about their own literacy skills? How do they and their parents get feedback on their progress? How do you see using a developmental continuum? Add your ideas to the calendar.

# Chapter 18

# What Do You See in a Classroom Devoted to Literacy Development?

| Questions to Ponder Before Reading |
| --- |

♦ What is your best memory of an observation of your teaching?

♦ What would your ideal observation be like?

♦ How would your teaching have been different if you had had someone come in every month to talk with you about your students?

Just as students need feedback, so do teachers. What do their classrooms say about the strength of their culture of literacy? Are the rules, roles, and rituals building children's confidence, interest, and knowledge of language? How much time is devoted to thinking, talking, reading, and writing? As a teacher, does his or her language focus on students developing as readers and writers? Is instruction systematic and just-in-time, based on a developmental continuum? Is assessment ongoing and in-depth, providing students with feedback and helping them reflect on their own about their progress? Do students see themselves as leaders in their own journey as readers and writers?

This chapter outlines what to look for in the planning, use of time, instruction, assessment, and student perceptions and behavior in the classroom, and suggests ways to observe and provide constructive feedback to teachers. Whether you are a principal, literacy coach, or a peer mentor, or are reflecting on your own practice, this chapter will provide some perspective on the facets of classroom culture that support literacy development and give you concrete ways to collect information on teaching and learning.

The diagram below provides an overview of how planning and classroom management flow out of being careful observers to assess what children can do. You can support this kind of learning environment by providing the time and tools for discussions about the developmental continuum, by shifting conversations away from labeling children to talking about what they can and can't do, and by talking about how they are using flexible groups to give students the opportunity to engage in meaningful, challenging tasks. Perhaps you can budget for classroom libraries, student journals and student book-making materials. You can encourage everyone to emphasize what students are doing well and to showcase their learning progress.

Every structure, every interaction, every expectation can express an inherent respect for how students are developing ways to make sense of the written word. In these classes you will hear self-correction, strategies for making meaning, and conversations about the content and processes of reading and writing. The routines provide time for reflection and conversation. The environment is rich with student writing, drawings, and responses to literature. There are lists of favorite words and strategies for comprehension.

You will notice in the diagram on page 165 that the assessment tools are the bookends of learning. The formal ones are examples of some that may be required in your school and often take months to get the results back to the teachers, students, and families. The informal tools are more like those that have been discussed so far because their results can be put to immediate use in the learning environment. For some, "diagnostic" has come to mean looking for weaknesses. Here it is used to refer to the process of identifying how children understand language as from the Greek words *dia* and *gnosis* meaning *by knowledge*. The diagnostic classroom environment revolves around the knowledge the teachers and students have about how children understand language.

## Planning

As already discussed, the goal of literacy development is for students to be strategic, confident, ready to learn, able to reflect, and able to develop knowledge through language. With these goals in mind, the majority of class time is devoted to students reading and writing, discussing what they are reading and writing about and talking about what they are discovering about how language works.

Planning for instruction and management of the classroom is based on creating time blocks for students to read and write independently and to interact with each other and the teacher. Diagnostic information is used to plan instruction. To keep students in a self-correcting mode, teacher feedback to students often takes the form of labeling strategies students are using and

# Developing a Culture of Literacy

Diagnostic Info

Independent activities

Whole group modeling

Small group discussion

**PLANNING**

Develop student profiles

Identify strategies students use

Plan instruction & interaction

Identify strategies to model and teach

**DIAGNOSTIC ASSESSMENT**

**Formal**
Developmental Reading Assessment (DRA) Comprehension

Observation Survey

DRA Attitudes and Preferences

Writing Prompts

**Informal**
Teacher Observation

Checklists based on developmental continuum

Anecdotes

**OUTCOMES ASSESSMENT**

**Formal**
Standardized tests of reading

(perhaps State Proficiency Tests)

Writing Prompts

**Informal**
Portfolios

Books read each year

Books written each year

Response journals

Able to reflect

Develop knowledge through reading & writing

Confident

**Outcome: Literate Students**

Strategic

Ready to learn

Balance and Flexibility

Whole groups

Small groups

Independent

**IMPLEMENTATION**

Student work displayed

Daily schedule

Favorite words & strategies posted

Student access to books and materials

**Literacy Rich Environment**

suggesting new strategies. In groups, small and large, students share the strategies they use to understand what they are reading.

Since students are moving at different rates through the continuum of skills and strategies, flexible grouping of students lets teachers teach new skills and strategies as they see students need them, as well as allot time for them to discuss their reading and writing with other students and the teacher.

To participate in a classroom based on these ideas, students need to understand the goals and what their roles are. These are related to the rights and responsibilities but are more specific. For example, students need to know we expect them to:

- ◆ Read every day for fun;
- ◆ Read every day to learn;
- ◆ Talk about what you are reading;
- ◆ Use language to think, communicate, and learn;
- ◆ Think about how language works while reading and writing;
- ◆ Talk about the strategies used to read and write;
- ◆ Notice the strategies other people use to read and write and adopt the ones you like;
- ◆ Ask for help with your reading and writing; and
- ◆ Talk about your writing.

Of course expecting these things, posting them, and talking about them is not enough. For students to take this much responsibility, the teacher must plan the time for individual reading and writing and conversation. The overall focus has to be on exploring ideas, listening to each other, and learning together. Instruction has to focus on modeling and coaching in strategies as children need them. Assessment is in service of facilitating conversations about learning, about diagnosis, and celebrating progress. These are the areas you can observe and give teachers options that will increase student involvement in their own literacy development.

## Use of Time

From "time on task" to the emphasis on "focused instruction" the use of time in the classroom has been talked about and researched for many years. Five, six or seven hours a day are spent in school. How many minutes are spent in giving directions, disciplining, or correcting students? How many minutes do students spend reading? Writing? Discussing? When you think of the time in terms of seconds and minutes, it's amazing how much time there is in a day! And there are so many options for how to use that time.

It's not just the amount of time, but the feel of the time. Group instruction can be fast-paced and engaging, slow and methodical, or "hurry up and wait." What is the pace of things? Who sets the pace? In small groups, children can pace off each other in highly focused discussions about something they have all read. When individual children have a clear purpose for their activities, they can pace themselves. Transitions can take a lot of time, or can be routine. We can't "make" time or "stop" time but we can certainly change our relationship with time to make it more productive and satisfying, as in the old adage, time "flies" when you are having fun. We've all had that experience of being so focused on something that we are unaware of time passing.

The first step is to become aware of how time is used in the classroom. You can sit in on the literacy block and code what you hear every five sec-

onds. This simple method provides a clear picture of how time is used. When I was in graduate school, I worked as an observer of innovative programs using Flanders Interaction Analysis Categories (FIAC)[1] to collect evidence of the teaching patterns that distinguish one program from another, and to use these data to help explain differences in outcomes from these programs. How teachers used time was a critical element in the shape of programs. I noticed that the teachers who had fast-paced intensive approaches with built-in rituals felt they had plenty of time to do things. Their students reported that these classes were easy to follow, and that they learned a lot. The fast pace within a familiar structure meant students could focus on learning.

Here's how it works. You code what happens every interaction or every five seconds such as who is talking (the teacher or the student) and the kind of talk (questions or statements, talking or listening, directions or lecture, praise, correcting, or clarifying). The categories can be created by the teachers, identified as part of professional development in particular strategies, or the ones suggested here adapted and extended from the FIAC.

---

1. See http://www.hebes.mdx.ac.uk/teaching/Research/PEPBL/methpap6.pdf for a study using FIAC to compare problem-based learning with other methodologies.

Consider these for observing whole-group instruction.

| Teacher talk | 1 | *Accepts or clarifies the feelings of a student* |
|---|---|---|
| | 2 | *Praises or encourages students actions or behavior* |
| | 3 | *Extends, builds on, or uses ideas of students* |
| | 4 | *Asks questions* |
| | 5 | *Lectures giving facts or opinions about content or procedures* |
| | 6 | *Gives directions* |
| | 7 | *Corrects students* |
| | 8 | *Modeling* |
| | 9 | *Gives students choices, as in, "What choice can you make to help you to learn better right now?" or "You can make a connection to your life or another story."* |
| Student talk | 10 | *Responds to teacher questions or prompts* |
| | 11 | *Expresses own ideas, asks thoughtful questions, initiates a new topic* |
| | 12 | *Silence or confusion* |
| | 13 | *Follows along, visually or orally as in reading a shared text or listens attentively* |

Whole-group literacy instruction is often for the purpose of modeling reading strategies. Enlarged text is used and students follow along with their eyes and voices at different times. The teacher may read aloud the text, stopping to think aloud to model how an active reader thinks while reading. Or, one text may be used for shared reading. The teacher chooses the text for a specific purpose such as to illustrate a structure or organization. By reading to and with the students, the teacher provides enough support so the text can be more complex and interesting than the students could read on their own.

The coding will reveal the patterns of listening and modeling, lecturing and criticizing, and the role of the students. Here's an example of the coding for a lesson in which the teacher has chosen a nonfiction passage about global climate change structured around questions and answers to read and discuss as a model for nonfiction writing. The passage is presented on an overhead transparency.

*Code*

5    *T: We've been talking about how to share what you learn in your investigations with people who know very little about the topics. Today I want to introduce you to the Q&A organization as a model of nonfiction writing.*

| | |
|---|---|
| 6 | T: I want everyone to squint so when you look at the front of the room, you see |
| 4 | large shapes rather than details. [puts up Q&A passage]. Now what shape is |
| | the passage? What is the visual structure? Discuss it and be ready to share in |
| | 30 seconds. [30 seconds] What do you notice? |
| 10 | S1: It looks like headings and paragraphs |
| 10 | S2: Like subheadings in a textbook |
| 10 | S3: Only the headings are questions |
| 4 | T: What does this structure tell you about what to expect when you read? |
| 10 | S5: The paragraph will answer the question |
| 11 | S6: I bet you can read the questions in any order you want! |
| 10 | S7: The questions and paragraphs are like separate ideas |
| 6 | T: Let's read and find out. |
| 13 | [teacher reads with students reading along out loud] |

---

**Do scientists agree about global warming?**
Scientists who study the climate are still arguing about how fast the earth is warming and how much it will warm, but they do agree that the earth is warming and that it will keep warming if we don't do anything about it.

---

*Code*

| | |
|---|---|
| 4 | T: Was it as you expected? Discuss it and be ready to share in 30 seconds. [30 |
| 6 | seconds] What do you say? |
| 10 | S5: Yes, the question and answer are about same thing. The answer is in the |
| | paragraph. |
| 11 | S9: And the answer is simple. I like that |
| 1 | T: So simple and to the point is something you like. |
| 3, 6 | What are some other good things about this organization that you notice |
| 4 | already? |
| | Discuss your ideas [30 seconds listening to students buzz about it] What are |
| | some advantages? |
| 10 | S12: The question gets you ready for the answer |
| 11 | S15: I like how the paragraph is really an answer to the question |
| 10 | S8: Since the question is on its own line so it stands out. It makes you stop |
| | and think about it for a minute before you read the paragraph |
| 3 | T: So advantages you see are ... [reads list she has made on the board] Let's see |
| 13 | if what you have noticed is a pattern. Let's read the next Q&A. [All read |
| | together out loud] |

> **What is causing global warming?**
> Scientists agree that the burning of fossil fuels like oil and coal cause green-house gases to escape into the air and that these gases are causing most of the warming. Another cause is deforestation (cutting down trees). Trees soak up carbon dioxide, one of the greenhouse gases, from the air.

*Code*

| | |
|---|---|
| 4 | *T: What do you think? Is the pattern the same? Discuss it and be ready to* |
| 6 | *share in 30 seconds. [30 seconds] What did you notice?* |
| 10 | *S16: The question keeps to the pattern—it's by itself and is something inter-esting and important to know.* |
| 10 | *S5: The paragraph answers the question. It gives causes for global warming.* |
| 11 | *S6: You could read this question before the other one* |
| 10 | *S20: It's a separate idea from the first one.* |
| 10 | *S24: It looked like the same pattern to us.* |
| 6 | *T: Okay, one more Q&A to confirm, and this time also think about what it* |
| 13 | *takes to write like this. [all read]* |

> **What is the difference between "global warming" and "climate change?"**
> "Global warming" refers to the increase of the earth's average surface tem-perature due to a build-up of greenhouse gases in the atmosphere. "Climate change" is a broader term that refers to long-term changes in climate, including average temperature and precipitation.

*Code*

| | |
|---|---|
| 4 | *T: Is the pattern the same? How many people think it is? [show of hands—all* |
| 10 | *raise hands]* |
| 4 | *T: So now, what do you think it would take to write like this? Discuss it and be* |
| 6 | *ready to share in one minute. [60 seconds] What do you think?* |
| 10 | *S25: You have to know what questions people would ask* |
| 10 | *S6: You would have to be sure your questions were separate—about different topics.* |
| 10 | *S22: You would want to write really clear short answers.* |
| 6 | *T: Okay, we have a pretty good idea of how this Q&A organization works for nonfiction writing. Take five minutes to describe it for yourself in your writer's notebook. Then jot down some ideas for Qs you might answer. Con-tinue to collect Qs as you work through the investigation and tell people about it. Find out what they would like to know. Good work analyzing this today.* |

An analysis of this shared reading lesson shows that the most frequent categories of teacher talk were asking questions and giving directions. The most frequent category of student talk was answering questions. The teacher established a pattern of getting the students to analyze the structure of the Q&A organization. This lesson could be followed by one in which the teacher models writing a Q&A. The objective of the lesson was met, but the teacher asked all the questions. Could the students ask the questions? Given the objective, what if the teacher started with just one question, "What do you need to know to be able to use the Q&A organization for your investigation?" The coding makes clear the pattern. She begins the discussion with what is, leading to a discussion of what could be, giving the students more responsibility for thinking about how they will use the structure in their own writing.

Summary of coding

| Teacher talk | 1 | 1 | Accepts or clarifies the feelings of a student |
|---|---|---|---|
| | 2 | | Praises or encourages students actions or behavior |
| | 3 | 2 | Extends, builds on, or uses ideas of students |
| | 4 | 7 | Asks questions |
| | 5 | 1 | Lectures giving facts or opinions about content or procedures |
| | 6 | 8 | Gives directions |
| | 7 | | Corrects students |
| | 8 | | Modeling |
| | 9 | | Gives students choices, as in, "What choice can you make to help you to learn better right now?" or "You can make a connection to your life or another story." |
| Student talk | 10 | 16 | Responds to teacher questions or prompts |
| | 11 | 4 | Expresses own ideas, asks thoughtful questions, initiates a new topic |
| | 12 | | Silence or confusion |
| | 13 | 3 | Follows along, visually or orally as in reading a shared text or listens attentively |

Since there are probably several activities going on at a time during a portion of the literacy block, I recommend coding the whole group modeling or shared experience, and then coding the small group instruction, and then the independent activities of students. For observing the small group, some categories are presented below to reflect the conversational nature of small group interactions.

| Teacher talk | 1 | Accepts or clarifies the feelings of a student |
| | 2 | Praises or encourages students actions or behavior |
| | 3 | Extends, builds on, or uses ideas of students |
| | 4 | Asks questions |
| | 5 | Lectures giving facts or opinions about content or procedures |
| | 6 | Gives directions |
| | 7 | Corrects students |
| | 8 | *Encourages or prompts students to comment on or extend each other's ideas* |
| | 9 | *Listens to students' ideas* |
| Student talk | 10 | Responds to teacher questions or prompts |
| | 11 | Expresses own ideas, asks thoughtful questions, initiates a new topic |
| | 12 | Silence or confusion |
| | 13 | *Responds to another student* |

In the small group interaction, you are looking for a different pattern of interaction; more discussion of content and strategy, more problem solving, and more listening on the part of the teacher to hear from the students how they are doing.

For independent work, consider coding the following:

| Teacher talk | 1 | Accepts or clarifies the feelings of a student |
| | 2 | Praises or encourages students actions or behavior |
| | 3 | Extends, builds on, or uses ideas of students |
| | 4 | Asks questions |
| | 5 | Lectures giving facts or opinions about content or procedures |
| | 6 | Gives directions |
| | 7 | Corrects students |
| | 8 | *Listens to student's ideas* |
| | 9 | *Labels the strategies a student is using* |
| Student talk | 10 | Responds to teacher questions or prompts |
| | 11 | Expresses own ideas, asks thoughtful questions, initiates a new topic |
| | 12 | Silence or confusion |

In independent activity, the emphasis is on listening to individual children's ideas, questions, and reading or reviewing their writing and giving them labels for the strategies they are using. Unlike the small-group situation, in the individual conference a student gets all the attention, can ask for specific help, and the teacher can make specific notes about the student's developmental progress. Sometimes these individual conferences can be as simple as updates on what the student is doing, but the goal is to have them be more substantive—more about what the student is thinking and reading or writing about.

At first, you may feel intimidated by the number of codes. Once you use them a couple of times, you will easily remember them. The most important thing is that you are objectively coding the interaction so you can use data for your discussion about a teacher's classroom practice. When used for this purpose, teachers really appreciate the information, since they, like their students, crave specific feedback. If the data are consistent with their intentions for their practice, the affirmation can lead to an expansion of the strategies a teacher uses. If there are discrepancies, the teacher can change things in her practice to be more in line with her intentions for how she wants things to go.

Don't hesitate to change the categories. As your faculty defines their vision for a culture of literacy and the teaching strategies that are aligned with it, other categories may emerge. When you are working with an individual teacher, ask her to review the categories and discuss what they mean to her. Modify, drop, replace, or add categories so the data is useful to her for thinking about her practice. The discussion is more important than the specific categories, since they will change with discussion and use. The discussion supports the teacher as a reflective practitioner and encourages the use of data and collaboration in the future.

## Focus

The coding method can be used to characterize the focus of a classroom. Consider shifting the categories to be about what the teacher and students are doing, rather than what they are saying:

1  Reading
2  Writing
3  Listening
4  Asking questions
5  Giving feedback
6  Giving information
7  Planning
8  Discussing
9  Presenting
10  Thinking out loud
11  Reflecting

What behaviors on this list would you predict you would see the most of in a classroom with a focus on evolving student understanding of language? Would teachers and students both be doing all these things? Would some be things only the teacher does? Some that only the students do? Some you would expect students to be doing most of the time? Some you would expect teachers to be doing most of the time?

In a culture of literacy, the focus is on supporting students in their activities to become good readers and writers. In a not so subtle shift, the class focuses on helping them, rather than controlling them or taking them through a series of activities that are have been shown to be "good for them." The curriculum is used as a resource *about* the sequence of learning, not *the* sequence. Instead, the sequence develops from the students' unfolding understanding of how print works. The teacher sees students as being on their own developmental paths and in need of expert assistance.

So in a culture of literacy, students are very active. When they are working independently, they have something they want to do that is important and that they feel capable of doing. They have a purpose and so make good use of their time. In small groups, students are prepared to discuss something they have previously read, or they come prepared to read together and discuss the characteristics of the text. They can tell you the purpose of any activity they are doing.

You can interview students about what they are doing to gauge the extent to which the culture is supporting their role in their individual development. As part of your observation ask students questions. Choose the students randomly before you go into the classroom and interview them quietly during independent time.

- What can you tell me about what are you doing right now?
- Why are you doing this? How is it helping you?
- What is interesting to you about what you are doing?
- What are your next steps?
- Are you a better reader than you were last year?
  - How do you know you are better reader? (if yes)
  - What do you plan to do to get better? (if no)
  - What did you do to get better?

Ask them about their small and large groups before and after they meet. Choose students randomly to get a better picture of the whole class across the range of students. Ask questions such as:

|             *Before*              |              *After*               |
| --------------------------------- | ---------------------------------- |
| What do you expect to do in this group? | What was different than you expected? |
| What do you expect to learn?      | What did you learn?                |
| How will you use what you have learned? | How will you use what you learned? |

You can ask the teacher similar questions about the focus of specific activities and of the classroom in general. For example, some questions and sample answers could be:

| *Questions to ask the Teacher* | *Possible Answers* |
| --- | --- |
| *How do students know what do to in any given activity?* | *For example, there's a pattern or I tell them each time* |
| *How do students know what they are doing well as readers and writers?* | *For example, they notice what works or I tell them* |
| *How would you say the students view their independent time, say while you are teaching a small group* | *For example, that they have assignments they need to complete, or as a time when they can read, write and think about things by themselves, with me or with other students.* |

The focus of the literacy classroom is on purposeful activity. Those purposes are equally known and valued by teachers and students alike. Students know why they are doing different activities so they can focus their attention and effort.

## Instruction

How can instruction be organized to involve students in focusing their attention on their own understanding? What roles and rituals can be built into lessons? What language and symbols keep the students in the driver's seat and open to learning new strategies for understanding and communicating. As has been discussed, the use of time is important: pacing; giving students more talk time; and using teacher talk time to clarify, label, and support students' unfolding understanding of language. The focus of the classroom needs to be on purposeful activity. If instruction is fast paced and purposeful, what else is there to consider? With these principles as the foundation of instruction, this section explores making instruction connected, planning for developmental needs, and being flexible and responsive in interactions with different size groups.

Instruction has been described as spiraling, sequential, or inquiry based. In the literacy classroom it is perhaps best described as "looping" since ideas  and discussions come back around in new contexts and at more sophisticated levels. Even the best readers and writers often consider their relationship with language one of visiting and revisiting, finding ways to understand and communicate anew with each project or text. "Iterative" is a word used in computer programming to describe functions that loop back on themselves, occurring at different phases of a program. With this looping in mind, instruction is always part of the larger conversation about how language works. It recalls prior conversations, and anticipates future ones. Nothing is taught in isolation, nor is there pressure to "complete" or "cover" something because this is the one and only time it will be addressed.

In planning, the teacher considers what strategies students are using and what they could benefit from next. She chooses texts to support modeling or instruction in those strategies. She thinks about how to call students' attention to the salient features of the texts to help them develop the strategies. Because she has internalized the developmental continuum, she thinks about her students and what they will understand about the strategy she is modeling or teaching. The strategy she had chosen is not one most students are able to use independently, so she will plan many different ways to engage them in thinking about it, using and noticing its important features.

Whole group instruction is usually for the purpose of modeling reading, writing or strategies more sophisticated than students can use on their own. Several nuances define the whole group instruction in a culture of literacy. The teacher appears to be sharing special information she has discovered and values. She is giving this "insider" knowledge as a gift to students because she wants them to have it and use it. There is a clear message that they are ready to hear it and ready to use it. The teacher is an expert; the kind of expert that knows what nonexperts don't get. She doesn't let them fall into the typical traps, or if she does, she gives them an escape route so they can navigate by themselves in the future.

When you observe a whole group lesson, you can use the coding system, or you write down phrases the teacher uses.

| What to look for | What the teacher says or does—examples |
| --- | --- |
| Introduces the text and the strategy | Remember that story we read about that boy's adventure in Italy? Remember how you liked the dialog because you knew what the characters were thinking and feeling? This book is about a girl's adventure in an amusement park. The story is told by a narrator who knows everything! An omniscient narrator, it's called. I think you will like it for the some of the same reasons you liked the use of dialog before. |
| Gets the students to attend to the relevant "cues" | See what you can find out from the narrator that you wouldn't otherwise know. Raise your hand when you hear some of that insider knowledge. [The teacher starts to read aloud from text on the overhead] When a student raises her hand, the teacher underlines the word. |
| Has them revisit the idea or strategy | [After a page, she pauses] Look at what we underlined. What do you notice about the kinds of information the narrator is giving you? [Repeats this for subsequent pages] Is there anything an omniscient narrator can't write about? |
| Checks in with them about their understanding | Why do you think this author chose to have an omniscient narrator? Teacher lists stories the class has read together, then asks, Which of these stories has an omniscient narrator? How do you know? Choose one story and tell why you think the author chose this strategy? |
| Connects with familiar texts | What other stories have you read with an omniscient narrator? [teacher lists them] |
| Connects with familiar strategies | Earlier, I reminded you how you like dialog. What is similar about dialog and an omniscient narrator as a strategy? |
| Looks to the future for connections and use of the strategies | When would you like to use the strategy of an omniscient narrator? Are there any story ideas you would like to revisit and use this strategy to redo them? Would you like to read more stories with this viewpoint? |

When you discuss these data with a teacher, the goal is to talk about what the teacher intended to do, and if what she did and said supported that intention. If a teacher says she has considered what students will find confusing, such as the kinds of things an omniscient author cannot describe, and she never says anything about that as a tricky thing, she has missed an opportunity. If there's no insider information, perhaps the teacher has not thought about the potential misconceptions. Or perhaps there's a need to discuss a way to focus students on the cues that is interesting. As with coded observations, the data is the starting point in talking about what happened in the class and how the culture reflects the intention to support students in becoming literate.

## Assessment

It is well-documented now that students who have clear tasks and get immediate, focused feedback make better progress than students who do not. In his 2006 book *Classroom Assessment and Grading That Work*, Robert Marzano,[2] summarizes research that shows that assessment affects achievement when it is positive, frequent, and based on clear goals and outcomes. In a classroom culture supporting literacy, the teacher needs to provide positive, frequent feedback based on goals and outcomes. Just as important, the teacher needs to set students up to get, give, and use feedback individually and in groups. This creates a multiplier effect on achievement since teacher-student interaction is supplemented by productive student self-talk and constructive student-student interaction. In this section, we describe how to observe the culture of assessment in a classroom.

In the literacy classroom, we want to see students who know what is expected, how progress is evaluated, and who engages in evaluative talk. If evaluation is transparent and collaborative in these ways, students will be more task-focused, content-focused and product-oriented which, in turn, leads to higher achievement. According to Dornbusch and Scott (1975),[3] "workers exert greater effort when they perceive evaluations are soundly

2. Marzano, R. (2006). *Classroom assessment and grading that work*. Alexandria, VA: ASCD.
3. Dornbusch, S. M., & Scott, W. R. (1975). *Evaluation and the exercise of authority*. San Francisco: Jossey-Bass.

based." Students as "workers" will also value evaluation that they think makes sense and will help them improve. The goal is for students to value the learning, understand the criteria to judge their progress, and to have opportunities to use the criteria to get feedback on their progress. The feedback loops that result help the student to become self-regulating (Capra, 1997)[4] both in the learning and in the use of what is learned later in other tasks. Modeling and coaching both contribute to establishing feedback loops. The model carries the criteria of the expected performance. Coaching, whether through self-talk or feedback from others, compares the current performance to the expected or desired performance. Effective learners seek and use feedback constantly to refine their performance.

What do you look for in assessment in the classroom? The task and the students' interaction are the focus. The more students talk and work together, the more they learn (Cohen, Lotan, & Holthuis, 1997).[5] The clearer they are about the task and the evaluation criteria, the more productive their talk is. The task should be:

1. Complex, requiring higher level thinking
2. Written down and visible so students can refer to it often
3. Have simple, clear evaluation criteria written for or to the students

For example, in groups, second graders read three different versions of *The Three Little Pigs*. The task is to create and act out their own versions that are different from any they have read. The skit should have good guys and bad guys, a problem between them that makes sense, and a series of events that lead to a solution to the problem. They should practice the skit and be prepared to do it more than once for different audiences. Notice the complexity of the task, "not like any of the versions you've read." (1) The task is posted on a poster in the drama center where the clothes, props, and masks are kept so it is always visible. (2) The evaluation criteria are simple and clearly written to the students so they can refer to them as they develop, dramatize, and practice their story. (3) Without the complexity, the criteria are unnecessary. A straightforward, right answer task doesn't need evaluation criteria. Without the evaluation criteria, students don't have a way to gauge and discuss quality, so their interactions are not focused on the task. At best, they are congenial and come to some agreement about what they want to do. At worst, they

---

4. Capra, F. (1997). *The web of life: A new scientific understanding of living systems.* New York: Anchor.

5. Cohen, E. G., Lotan, R. A., & Holthuis, N. C. (1997). Organizing the classroom for learning. In E. G. Cohen & R. A. Lotan (Eds.), *Working for equity in heterogeneous classrooms: Sociological theory in practice* (pp. 32-43). New York: Teachers College Press.

argue and struggle for power to control the direction of the group. With clear evaluation criteria that the students are responsible for using they can focus on working together to accomplish the task. The shift in responsibility from the teacher giving feedback to students using the criteria to shape what they are doing improves the quality and quantity of their interactions with each other.

*If you can read this book, thank a teacher!*

The second part of observing assessment focuses on the student-student interaction. How much and the kind of interactions students have is a strong indicator of the effectiveness of assessment. In a culture of literacy, students are leaders in the learning process. They all participate, taking turns in leadership roles, and ultimately actively seeking and using feedback to learn.

For example, while the teacher has a small group at the table in the corner for a discussion of the stories and texts they have read about swamps, the rest of the class are organizing themselves for discussions of their independent reading books. The routine is for students to sit together in pairs for a "book talk" in which they discuss what each of them is reading. First, they make a plan for how they are going to talk about their books. A running list of ways to talk about books is posted, so several of the pairs of students are looking at it and discussing what they will do. The list has ideas such as:

- ♦ Why you chose this book;
- ♦ What you know about the author and why he or she wrote this book;
- ♦ How the book is organized;
- ♦ How the author gets your attention in the beginning;
- ♦ Connections between the book and your life, the book and other books, or the book and life in general;
- ♦ Why you would or would not recommend this book to someone else and who you think would like it;
- ♦ The language in the book—how the author uses language; and
- ♦ What you are learning from this book about writing, about the topic about the author, or about yourself.

Within a couple of minutes, the pairs have settled down to talking about their books. They take turns discussing one book, then the other. They ask each other questions, check to be sure they understand, and show interest in the book by leaning over, reading sections of it, and listening to each other. Another poster describes, "How to have a good book talk" with evaluation criteria like:

♦ Make a plan;

♦ Show you are interested by leaning forward, looking the other person in the eye, and asking questions that get them to talk more;

♦ Refer to the book to explain what you are thinking. Use the text to help the other person understand your ideas and the book; and

♦ Talk about how your book talk went.

You can code these student-student interactions in much the same way you coded the lessons, coding who is talking and the kind of talk. The categories reflect the criteria. For example:

| Code | Kind of talk |
|------|--------------|
| 1 | Planning, talking about how to talk or work together, or what to do |
| 2 | Talking about the book |
| 3 | Pointing out specific passages, words, or pictures in the book |
| 4 | Asking questions about the book |
| 5 | Asking questions about the other students' thoughts, feelings, ideas, etc. |
| 6 | Thinking out loud |
| 7 | Answering questions |
| 8 | Discussing—rapid give and take |
| 9 | Disengaged—off task |
| 10 | Waiting for an adult |
| 11 | Reflecting on what and how they have talked |

In the situation described, you can see that categories 9 and 10 would seldom be used in a culture of literacy since it is difficult for students to disengage when there are only two of them if the task is clear, and they have no need to wait for an adult if they understand the criteria for evaluating success. You should expect to see a good balance of talking and listening in the pair's discussion of their books as an indication of strong task focus.

As is suggested by the "book talk" activity, one of the best times to look at the use of assessment in the classroom is when students are working independently. Without the direction of the teacher, it becomes clear rather quickly whether or not the culture puts students in a leadership role in directing, completing, and evaluating their own work. Another method for collecting data is to scan the room and count how many students are engaged in each different kind of task. How many are:

| How many students | Activity |
|---|---|
| | Reading |
| | Writing |
| | Student-student discussion—rapid give and take |
| | Teacher-student interaction |
| | Thinking |
| | Asking questions |
| | Listening |
| | Procedural—returning books, getting paper |
| | Disengaged—off task |
| | Waiting—standing in line, waiting for a turn |
| | Reflecting on what and how they have talked |

What about teacher assessment in a culture of literacy? You have seen how shifting responsibility to students for judging their work changes their use of time and their interactions. Teachers can magnify the effect of their interactions with students by offering sound feedback. In a summary of major reviews of research, Marzano defines sound feedback as:

♦  Frequent;
♦  Gives students a clear picture of their progress on learning goals;
♦  Gives students a clear picture of how they might improve; and
♦  Encourages students to improve.

To gauge the nature of teacher feedback, talk with the teacher about his or her intentions and plans for feedback. Then observe the teacher for feedback, coding only the amount and nature of the feedback. For example, you can simply count the number of times a teacher provides feedback to students in a given period of time in a particular kind of lesson. Then you can code the feedback as meeting or not meeting the criteria for sound feedback. Consider the following example from an observation during independent reading and morning conference time.

*The teacher moves around the room talking with individual students one at a time about what they are reading, the strategies they are using, what they are learning, and so forth. The teacher bends down to talk with a student and says, "I see you are reading another book about lizards. You really like lizards, don't you? How many books have you read about lizards now?"*

| Feedback | Clear Picture of Progress | Encouragement to Improve |
|---|---|---|
| *You've really learned a lot from all the books you have read on lizards* | You are learning more because you are reading more | Keep up the good work |

*The student responds that he has indeed learned a lot from books but also from having his own pet lizard. The teacher asks about the pet lizard.*

| Feedback | Progress | Encouragement |
|---|---|---|
| *Some time do you think you could bring in your pet lizard and share what you know with the class?* | You are an "expert" on lizards | Other students would be interested |

*There are a lot of big scientific words in these books. (student nods) "What do you do when you come to a big scientific word that you aren't quite sure what it means?" Student responds, "Well, I know most of the words because I read about lizards all the time, but if I don't know a word, I look it up or ask someone."*

| Feedback | Progress | Encouragement |
|---|---|---|
| *Those are good strategies* | You are reading books with scientific vocabulary | You are using good strategies to figure out what those words mean |
| *Do you ever read the words around the word you are trying to figure out? (student, "no") Do you think you might try that strategy sometime? (student, "yes")* | This strategy might work for you | You can do it |

## Summary

The rules, roles, rituals, symbols, and language in the classroom create the classroom culture in small yet powerful ways. You can tease these out in the open by observing the fine-grained details of tasks and interactions. Coding what is happening every few seconds creates data that tell the story of who is talking, thinking, and directing the learning.

## Reflection

This chapter is really about giving and receiving feedback as educators. Being able to collect data on instruction and its effect on students is part of being a faculty that is a community of learners. Just as students need to "own" the evaluation criteria that let them become self-regulating, so do teachers. Think about the feedback you give and have received in your learning. What has been the most helpful? The least helpful? Do students in your school have access to the criteria on which their progress is evaluated? Do they see those criteria as something they can use themselves and with each other? How can you make sound feedback an integral part of the learning process in your school? Add your ideas to the plan book.

# Chapter 19

# How Do You Involve Families and the Community?

**Questions to Ponder Before Reading**
- What do you remember about reading and writing with your family?
- What did they believe about literacy development?
- What is the best family activity you have ever participated in? What made it so good?
- What would you have liked to have your family do around literacy?

This book is about creating and sustaining such an intense culture of literacy in a school community that it affects the other 14-18 hours of the child's life. As a school leader you can model, support, cajole, and encourage literacy in a thousand small ways during the six hours they are in school. But you can extend your reach far beyond that time by making parents, families, and caregivers your partners in empowering students through reading and writing. Because you reach out to everyone in the school community all day long in large and small ways, you have many, many opportunities to make a difference. Your intention to promote reading and writing can permeate everything you do. Some people will notice, others will be influenced without really knowing it. To parents you are a leader. They look to you as an example, and as someone who can provide support and solve problems their children encounter in learning.

Your partners are parents, teachers, community members, and the students themselves. Your role in this partnership is to weave the members of the community into a fabric of literacy that surrounds students so no matter where they turn the people in their lives are expecting and supporting them in using language well for learning and communicating. Everywhere they turn, people should be asking them what they see, hear, and think, what they are reading about, what they are writing about, how they are feeling about their writing, and what their goals and choices are. The opportunity you have is to create this larger sense of community that takes on a life of its own because it has invented and reinvented itself over time to support its children in becoming literate.

Every month, you can host have a family read-in where families learn strategies for building a culture of literacy as part of their family life. This is a terrific tradition that can grow over time, including more and more parents, grandparents, cousins, babysitters, and other extended "family" members. In the month-by-month activities, you will find letters to send home to parents about the monthly theme and family night activities. This section describes some of the strategies you can use. As you try them out, you and the faculty will have other ideas for fun literacy activities for "Family Read-In" night. Plan them once a month as a way for families to learn fun and powerful ways to interact with each other. For each of the activities below, a format is suggested along with the activities. You will adapt these to best fit your setting and school community. If you can get free books, consider having a book swap or giveaway at each Family Read-In to increase the excitement. Letters to send home about Family Nights for each month are provided in Part II.

## Read to Each Other

There are so many times during the day that families can boost literacy skills in their children. In education, these are sometimes called sponge activities, since they soak up the time that is usually wasted with learning activities. Those minutes really add up and become fun ways to play with words and ideas, review skills, and ask questions.

For Family Read-In night, have lots of fun short pieces for families to read. At each table have poems, short stories, limericks, and jokes of different reading levels. Families take turns reading at the table, like they could at meals, in the car, and at family gatherings. Have things to read, rap, and sing. Give each family a packet to get them started, and recommend books, magazines, and student newspapers to read from.

Ideas:

+ *Where the Sidewalk Ends*, by Shel Silverstein
+ *The Adventures of Captain Underpants*, by Dav Pilkey
+ *American Girl* book series, by Susan Adler et al.

- Any work by Dr. Seuss
- *Curious George*, by Margret and Hans Augusto Rey
- *The Mitten*, by Jan Brett
- *Where the Wild Things Are*, by Maurice Sendak
- *Magic School Bus* series by Joanna Cole
- *Science Verse*, by Jon Scieszka

Some examples and places to get more ideas

- **http://www.magickeys.com/books/**
  Online stories for technology-oriented students
- **http://www.nea.org/readacross/resources/kidsbooks.html**
  NEA's "Kid's top 100 books"
- **http://www.randomhouse.com/rhpg/promos/greatbooks/booklist.html**
  Books specific for girls
- **http://kids.nypl.org**
  New York Public Library site has link to kids books
- **http://www.ucalgary.ca/~dkbrown/lists.html**
  University of Calgary's list of kid books by recommendation and subject area
- **http://www.monroe.lib.in.us/childrens/booklists/children_booklists.html**
  The Monroe County Public Library in Indiana provides an extensive list with information on reading levels and interest levels

# Read Together

When an adult reads with a child, especially with beginning readers, the child gets to see what to aim for. The adult is the up-close and personal model of easy reading—when you know almost all the words almost all the time, and you can read it so it makes it easier to understand just by the way you read it. Children

*We should read for power.*
*The book should be a ball of light in one's hand.*
—Ezra Pound

love to be read to, and easily mimic the adult. Reading together is like reading aloud, except you involve the child in whatever part of the reading they can do. It might be the child can read the repetitive phrases in the story, or "read" the pictures, or tell you what just happened on that page, or what they think will happen next. Since reading is mainly thinking, these conversations show the child how good readers think when they are reading.

For the Family Read-In, have reading materials and different ways of reading together at each table.

- Read every other line
- Read every other page
- Read together at the same time—choral reading
- One person "reads" the pictures, the other reads the words aloud
- One person reads aloud and the other one thinks about it and retells it in his or her own words
- One person reads the whole piece, then the other reads it
- Read dialog in roles
- One person reads, the other acts out what is happening
- The two people take turns reading and predicting what will happen next
- Take turns reading and drawing what is happening

## Talk About What You Read

I remember my father talking about sailing, sailboats, sailing trips, sailing gear—anything and everything sailing. He was always reading a book, or a magazine, even catalogs. Even though he only sailed a few weeks a year, he read about sailing all year long. He made lists, planned projects, picked out gadgets and planned trips. He talked about what he was reading and learning along the way. He would say, "Listen to this, daughter!" with great excitement.

Sometimes parents don't think their children will be interested in what they are interested in. The "kid culture" of television, toys, and movies that has been marketed to children and all of us is no real match for the excitement of an adult talking about what he or she cares about.

Encourage the parents and caregivers of your students to talk about what they are reading. For a Family Read-In have children bring the books they are reading and do book talks for the adults, and parents bring what they are reading to talk about. Set it up like a poster session, with parents and children at different tables for 10 minutes to do two or three book talks, and then be able to go to other people's talks. Encourage parents to talk about the things they are interested in and show the kinds of printed matter they read, like books, magazines, and newspapers.

## Art and Literature

Celebrate illustrations at a family night. Display the Caldecott Award books from your media center. The Caldecott Medal[1] was named in honor of nineteenth-century English illustrator Randolph Caldecott and is awarded annually by the Association for Library Service to Children, a division of the American Library Association, to the artist of the most distinguished American picture book for children.

Have children prepare to share their favorite illustrated books by reading parts of the story and showing the pictures. Have other children illustrate their favorite books and share the illustrations. Depending on how many children you have, you may want them to stand or sit around the room so families can circulate and talk with them about the illustrations in their books.

## Improvisation

This is the night where the actors and actresses get to shine. Have some students prepare to act out a poem or very short story while another student reads aloud. Then make it improvisation time. At each table have a book and a few props to act out the story or poem. Wrap up the evening with a few volunteers performing in front of the whole group.

## Quiz Show Night

Put a short story, poem, or newspaper article at each table with the following questions:

♦ What does this remind you of?
♦ What would you tell someone this is about?
♦ What do you notice about how it is written?

---

1. For more information, see http://www.ala.org/ala/alsc/awardsscholarships/literaryawds/caldecottmedal/caldecottmedal.htm

- ◆ What is the author's purpose?
- ◆ How would you improve on this?

Provide a scorecard with the names of the readings listed. Hand out the score cards at the entrance. When a family sits down at the table, they all read the story, taking turns or sitting together. Then one person takes the Q&A folder and asks the other family members the questions. The Q&A person gives approval for the answers and gives the readers credit on their scorecard for each question. The family keeps the scorecard with the list of readings and the questions at the top to add to at home.

## Favorites

Set up the tables for this night with different topics of each table and one color crayon, marker, or stamp at each one.

### Topic Ideas

| | |
|---|---|
| Color | Shoes |
| Story | Adventure |
| Food | Weather |
| Piece of clothing | Store |
| Sport | Time of day |

Families get a blank book, folded and stapled like a 5" × 8" program with a construction paper cover. Kids and adults create the cover page and introduction together. At each table, there are books, stories and poems about the topic. The adults write their favorite thing for the category and why on the left hand page, and kids write their favorite and why on the opposite page. They read them to each other. For example, "I love YELLOW because it is the color of the sun. It makes me smile. I feel warm and happy when I see yellow. I always choose the yellow marker in games too."

## Poetry for Dessert

Invite children to write their own poems, or read their favorites at an evening event. Choose a variety of ages and subjects. Invite parents to read poetry too. Make copies of the poems for the poets to give out at their tables. Start the evening off with a couple of poems for the whole group, then position the poets at a table in shifts so they are reading for 5-10 minutes, then joining the listeners.

Send home a collection of poems and a list of sources for poetry on a variety of subjects. Put a poem in your weekly newsletter. Post one in the hall with copies to take as parents stop into school. Remind families to have poetry for dessert as often as possible.

Resources:

◆ **http://www.Poetry.com**
A huge site nearly endless poetry choices

◆ **http://www.Gigglepoetry.com**
A fun poetry site mostly for kids and fun

There are also many online lesson plan sites that offer poetry lesson ideas such as:

◆ Poetry Class: http://www.poetryclass.net/resource.htm
◆ Teach-nology: http://www.teach-nology.com/teachers/lesson_plans/language_arts/poetry/
◆ Favorite poem project: http://www.bu.edu/favoritepoem/forteachers/lessonplans.html

## Grandparents as Storytellers

Storytelling needs new venues. Front porches and campfires are often few and far between, so make a Family Read-In a front-porch night where elders from the community come in and tell stories about when they were children; about the good ol' days. Encourage the storytellers to tell their favorite stories about growing up, the town, or other adventures. Anything goes!

In our town we have a furniture store that specializes in rockers. If you can get rockers for this family night, you can create a terrific storytelling environment. If not, make a cozy settings for storytelling by grouping four or five chairs in a small circle. Serve hot chocolate and cookies. Recruit grandparents and other "elders" from the community to tell stories 5-10 minutes in length. Let families move from one story circle to the next when you ring a gentle bell. If the story ends before the bell, have the storytellers encourage the story listeners to share what the story reminded them of or to ask questions.

A bonus of this evening could be capturing the stories on videotape to make a community collection.

## Business Partners

Ask local businesses to support building children's personal libraries. They can make outright donations, buy books from a list you provide, or purchase sets of books for the monthly school read-in (books are listed in the month-by-month activities). Larger companies may also ask employees to bring in used books to pass on. Having books related to the different businesses is sometimes appealing.

Have a Family Read-In with local business people bringing things to read about and from their businesses. At each table, have a representative from the business with menus, advertisements, business plans, and other reading materials. Ask them to talk about the purpose of each piece, who wrote it, who reads it, and the ideas behind the content and design. Have families move from table to table with a "shopping list" like the mall maps. Encourage the businesses to give away printed matter, business cards, or other printed materials.

## Community Organizations as Partners (Informal, Faith-Based, Service)

Encourage community organizations to have family literacy nights with their groups and in their locations. They can host book groups, book talks, author nights, read alouds, storytelling, writing contests, and poetry readings. These events can be in the child's first language and in their neighborhoods. At these events, children see adults valuing language and encouraging them to read and write.

## Summary

Family nights need to provide models and practice for simple, yet powerful ways children and their parents or caregivers can interact around reading and writing. Through these family nights, you are helping to develop the rituals and language that families need to focus on literacy. You are helping them develop a culture of literacy at home. The symbols of that culture are lots of things to read and bookshelves or other spaces dedicated to books. The rituals of the family literacy culture are activities such as making time to read, talking about what family members are reading, reading interesting passages aloud to each other, going to the library, and reading together. The language of family culture is supportive, curious, and connective. People don't make judgments, but rather listen carefully, ask questions and offer connections to their own lives, experience and reading.

## Reflection

How does your school involve families? What are your most successful parent-involvement activities? What makes these successful? How can you migrate these key elements of success over to a family read-in night? Some schools offer food, giveaways, have special guests, or involve their parent organization in the planning. Think about what you can do to have regular frequent family nights focused on literacy.

# Chapter 20

# How Do You Immerse Students in Literacy Through What They See and Hear Every Day?

<hr>

### Questions to Ponder Before Reading

◆ Close your eyes and take a mental walkthrough of your school. Jot down what you see in the entryway, the halls, your office or classroom, the cafeteria. What you do see, smell, and hear?

◆ Read through your list, then ask yourself, "How does this place feel? Friendly? High-pressured? Boring?" How would you like it to feel?

<hr>

Remember the alphabet cards over the chalk or white board in your first grade classroom? Did you see it in your mind's eye when I asked? Chances are you have a vivid visual memory for those green alphabet cards over the blackboard. Do you remember where you sat in first grade? Who you sat behind? The route you took to school? Do you remember how your school smelled when you walked in the door? Sensory memories are powerful and long-lasting and are a strong part of the culture. This chapter is about how to create a powerful physical culture for learning.

What do your students see every day when they first enter your school? What greets them in their classrooms? What do your teachers see when they enter your office? What adorns the walls in the faculty room? What do parents see when they enter the school office? You can consciously create an environment that teaches core strategies, encourages questioning, and builds enthusiasm for using language.

We are kinesthetic creatures; absorbing the sights and sounds around us. We are social creatures; endlessly curious about each other and prone to interaction. We are emotional beings; drawn to beauty and truth, repelled by violence, frightened by inconsistency and harshness. We are intellectual powerhouses; provoked by ideas, challenged by different perspectives, drawn to conundrums and always pattern-seeking. As a leader, you can create a safe, fun and exciting environment that will nurture language development through all these avenues.

Post it! Print it! Say it! Sing it!

## Meet a Reader, Writer, or Thinker

LISTENING

There is nothing like meeting an author, talking with him or her about the writing process, where ideas come from, and how the writing actually gets accomplished. The "live" experience of begin able to interact adds intensity and personalizes the experience. Librarians often bring in authors, but they also share their love of reading by sharing the books they have read. Their students experience the book through their eyes, the intonation in their voices, the connections they make to their own lives. Their enthusiasm is contagious. Sharing in another person's experience is both inviting and informative. For all these reasons, invite readers, writers, and thinkers from outside your school to spend time enriching your culture.

When you can't invite real people in, you can always invite virtual people, icons, or ideas. You can post symbols that invite thinking such as a light bulb, Rodin's Thinker, or Einstein. Invite students to make connections. With your virtual visitors, you are sending the message that ideas are important; big ideas by important thinkers, and students ideas in the form of their comments. Below are some examples of line drawings. Actual sizes are five by seven feet.

## Every Day Message on Chart Paper

When you enter the school, what do you see? If it is the same thing every day, people don't see it at all after the first few days. You can set the tone for thinking by printing a message on poster paper and posting it on an easel in the foyer. You can make it about upcoming events or special people, or highlighting an idea or one of the quotations about literacy in this book. You can

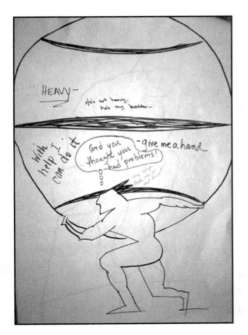
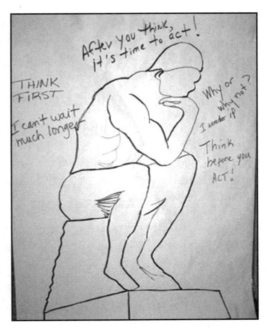

use it to provoke people to think about the shared mission of educating all our children. For example:

St. Augustine once wrote, "I learned most not from those who taught me, but from those who talked with me." In our school we both teach and listen, talk and question, converse and argue because it is all our ideas that make us the community we are. Have a conversation with one of our students today!

Or this example:

SPEAKING

"I have learned to create the conditions that make it possible for me to write badly without feeling badly about it … to write fast enough to outrun my internal critic … and to maintain the illusion that the only audience for my writing is me." Bruce Ballenger wrote a whole book called, *The Importance of Writing Badly*. In our school everyone writes as a way to share what we think and know. Sometimes we polish and publish what we write. Other times we write just for fun. Take time to write today!

## Post Visuals of What is Important

Remember the alphabet over the blackboard. Put the big ideas in front of everyone as much as possible. Here's a model of what it means to be literate that you can print out, enlarge, or recreate for a bulletin board, a newsletter, or a presentation. Combine a graphic like the one on the next page with text such as the following:

Be strategic. Learn what to do when they get stuck on a word, how to figure out an author's purpose and different ways to write a persuasive essay.

Reflect on what you might find out in reading by asking questions. Take time to reflect on what you just read to make connections. Reread and think about what you have written to hear your own thoughts in a different form. Reflect back to someone what they just said to see if you heard what they meant to say.

Develop your knowledge through reading and writing: learn to read and read to learn, collect books, articles, Web sites and videos on interesting ideas, write about what you are interested in, connect the ideas that intrigue you.

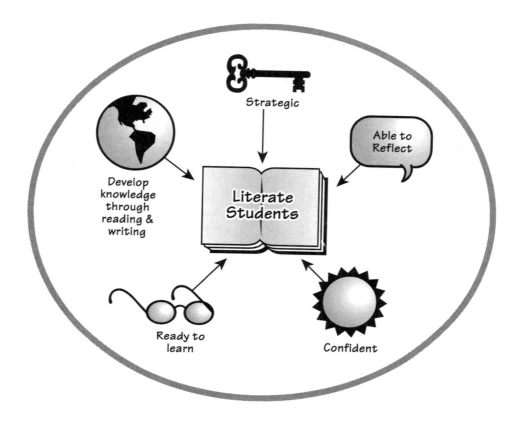

Read to learn. Be curious about everything. Keep an open mind. Listen well. Check your own understanding with those who know more than you. Share what you learn so others share with you.

Be confident. You have already learned to speak and understand the people around you. Do what you can do to the best of your ability and know that it is exactly what you need to be doing right now. When something is difficult, choose to struggle with it, knowing that you will understand it sooner rather than later.

## Story Map the Book of the Month

Encourage multiple visions and versions of story maps for the book of the month. Introduce different ways of mapping the structure of a book so students see them over and over again for different books. Use some standard maps, but praise the completely original "mind maps" that make a student's thinking visible. When I was working with the Department of Education in

Singapore around visual thinking, they told me they had given students visual maps to use, and they had quickly become bored with them. When we reintroduced mapping to students as a tool for making *their* thinking visible, they were excited to use mapping. For example, here are two different maps for *Oh, the Places You'll Go!* by Dr. Seuss. The standard map on the right shows comprehension and could be completed by all the students. The map below is unique, created by one mind interacting with the text and making it visible.

**Beginning**

The character starts off because it is his day. He makes choices about where to go and leaves the city to "wide open air."

**Middle**

The character has grand adventures. Things start to happen and he is happening too. He flies to great heights, then gets hung up in a tree and has a slump. He gets confused, finds himself in a waiting place, then escapes to a place where bands are playing. He's on TV, then finds himself alone, is scared and faces his problems.

**End**

The author reminds the character that "Life's a Great Balancing Act", so even if you get mixed up, you will succeed, so start climbing mountains.

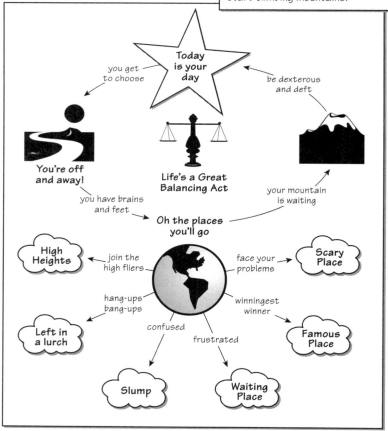

# Read Aloud in Morning Announcements

Like song, the "word" read aloud becomes music to the ears and to the heart. The reader adds his or her gift of voice and expression, of smiles and knowing eyes to the words carefully crafted by another.

Every week, if not every day, read something aloud as part of morning and afternoon announcements. Put something in the teachers' mailboxes that they can read aloud. Make the sound of language—beautiful, melodic language—part of what is heard in your school every day in many ways. Read short poems, quotations, or "teasers" from stories. You can read some of them yourself, but involve students and teachers in both selecting and reading them. For example, in September, read about beginnings.

On the task of beginning, writer Bernard Malamud said, *"Once you've got some words looking back at you, you can take two or three—or throw them away and look for others."* So just get a few words down and you are on your way!

In the month-by-month activities, morning announcement read alouds are suggested for the monthly theme. If your have other school themes, use them to read aloud something worth hearing. Share them in writing in the daily bulletin or print them out for a notebook in the office or library. The best way to tell if you are making good choices is if people ask for copies.

# Read With Students

Model reading aloud by picking a class to read aloud in every week. Have a favorite book in hand and drop into a class. Post a sign in the entrance to the school that says what book you are reading each week, and what class you will stop into to read portions of it. Leave the book with the class at the end of the week to read together or let students who are interested pick it up to read. Talk about why you like the book, how you found it, what you particularly like about the passages you choose to read aloud, and how it relates to your life, or other books you have read. If you have the budget or can get a sponsor such as a local bookstore, give the copy you have been reading to a student in the class for his or her home library. The new owner of the book can be chosen based on his or her written response to the book, another story inspired by the book, or even a sequel. Write a note in the beginning of the book from you to the student about what you both liked about the book to make it a cherished possession.

Have students read to you in your office. You can set it up so teachers send you students each day you are in the building. Each class has a week a month they can send students. If you can't set a specific time, just stop into the class to collect the student. Walk them to your office or the library, talking about the book and their reading and writing in general. As you listen to them read, notice several things they are doing well, and let them know afterwards in writing.

```
Thank you _____
For reading from _____
    I really like how you ___
                   _____
    Signed_____Date_____
```
Keep up the good work!

Thank you <u>Evan Petornell</u> for reading from <u>The Lion, the Witch and the Wardrobe</u>.

I really like how you *knew the characters really well and helped me to know them too.*

Signed: <u>Mr. Tabor</u>   Date: <u>Jan. 5, 2007</u>

## Summary

Close your eyes and envision your first school. Can you remember how the school felt as you walked in the door, the smells, the first thing you saw? These memories are powerful and clear today because they are rich in sensory details. Consider what memories your students are making as they enter the building, sit in their classroom and go through the day. Are they meeting writers, readers, or thinkers either real or imagined? We all take a look at our surroundings, scanning for what is there. Having an ever changing message board at the entrance to the school sets young minds in motion, reading aloud triggers thoughts, posting visuals of what is important develops the community values. Reading with students establishes the importance of reading to students and adults alike. Together these continue to build the culture of literacy.

## Reflection

Take a walk through the school with a child's eyes. What is vibrant, persistent, intriguing, or important? If you fast forwarded 20 years, what would your child's eyes remember? What would you like that late 20 something to remember? Reflect on what you really like about the visual world of your school and what you would like to change.

# Chapter 21

# How Do You Celebrate Speaking and Listening?

---

### Questions to Ponder Before Reading

♦ What do you remember reading aloud when you were a child in school?

♦ When and how do students talk about what they are reading in your school?

♦ What happens to student writing? Is it published? Posted? Sent home?

---

The spoken word with all its intonation, rhythm, and expression connects people or pushes them apart. While words on the page can seem flat and expressionless, seldom is the spoken word delivered without emotion. While you have developing readers and writers, most of your students can speak. Encourage thoughtful, playful, and purposeful speaking and listening whenever and wherever you can.

## Talk About Your Own Reading and Writing

Are you a reader and writer? Do you share your love of reading and writing with teachers, students, parents, and community? Do you read to learn? Do you talk about what you learn through reading? Do you write to your students and staff? Do they hear your author's voice? What are you reading this week? Once a week, share what you are reading that is interesting to you on the announcements. The other four days a week, have faculty, students, staff, and parents/community members share something they are reading and what it means to them.

# Feature Student Authors

Make it a point to hear from authors in your midst. Schools often have published authors come to visit, talk about their writing and do writing workshops. What about using the authors in your midst to do the same thing? Have student authors visit other classes to talk about stories they have written, how they got their ideas, and the strategies they used while they were writing. Set it up so students from different grade levels hear from each other. In the beginning, use a set of standard topics for the author and questions from the audience.

| Author's Role |
| --- |
| ◆ Read the story, poem or other work aloud |
| ◆ Tell where the idea came from |
| ◆ Describe how the story is structured |
| ◆ Talk about what was easy and what was hard in the writing |
| ◆ Ask for feedback in a specific area |

The rules of thumb for the author talks are that the author is in control of what feedback is given and how it is used. In other words, the author asks for feedback in areas s/he wants and then uses that feedback if it accomplishes a goal s/he has.

| Audience's Role |
| --- |
| ◆ Read the story ahead of time or follow along while it is being read |
| ◆ Ask: "How is this like or different than other things you have written?" |
| ◆ Ask: "What do you like best about this piece of writing?" |
| ◆ Ask: "What ideas do you have for your future writing?" |
| ◆ Offer feedback if asked by the author |

This is only a beginning for your homegrown author discussions. In the beginning, formality and structure are effective ways to make sure the discussions are positive. As students participate, they learn how to be both the author and the audience member, and can expand their questions or focus them more closely on what they need as an author, or what they want to know as an audience member. Collect their questions and post them as options for future author talks. With older students, set up groups of audiences of four or five with one author.

Remember, your job as a school leader is to make this kind of activity easy and effective for everyone so there is support and excitement to buoy it up. People need both the confidence and the know-how to participate. They learn this through seeing it in action and then participating. You can provide this through modeling with one class and having them model it for other classes, by modeling it in a faculty meeting and asking each teacher to schedule it, or by having it as an afterschool or evening activity. You may end up using all these strategies for creating success, or only one. You will quickly be able to see what support will be needed for this activity and others to gain momentum. Whole-school activities need champions. You can be the champion in the beginning, and usually someone else will take over that role, or everyone will be able to carry on after the first time so all you have to do is schedule it and remind people of what worked.

## Feature Teacher Authors

Do you have teachers who tell stories or write stories? Find the closet poets in your midst and give them your community's attention as their own small place in the sun. Their stories can be nonfiction or descriptive writing about their hobbies, passions, or families. Make authoring the norm rather than the exception so there are many models and many audiences. Make your school a place where familiar people draw on their own experiences to write for each other.

## Find the Writers in Your Community

Do you have writers in your community? Look around for journalists, technical writers, researchers, people who put out newsletters for their organizations, preachers who write sermons, restaurant owners who write menus, military employees who write manuals or directions, politicians who write speeches or position papers, lawyers who write briefs, or doctors, nurses, and medical technicians who write reports. Put out a call to your community, "Looking for writers to talk with students." Contact them directly and brief them on what you are looking for. Ask them to talk about how they write and who reads it.

---

### Questions for Visiting Writers

- How do you figure out what to write about? Are you assigned topics?
- If not, where do you get ideas for what to write about? How do you narrow down those ideas or select among them?
- How do you develop ideas? Through research? Interviews? Talking with people? From your imagination?
- How do you refine what you write? How do you edit your own work? Who else edits it?
- Who reads what you write? How do you know what they think of it?

---

You can prepare your visiting writers by talking over their answers to these questions to assure them that what they are sharing will be valuable to the students. To prepare the faculty and students for the visit, share the writer's answers to the questions. If possible, share some examples of the writing. If the writing is easy enough for students to actually read, giving students examples ahead of time allows them to ask very specific questions about the author's techniques and topics. For example, local papers have writers who look into the history of things great and small. For example, one local writer may have a folksy way of telling stories about people and places while getting all the history in. Here's a passage like that:

Francis made her living on egg farm (December 30, 2005)

Augusta Francis was born to Alonzo and Ella Francis in August of 1887. In 1894, she moved with her family to the little poultry farm on Annaquatucket Road that her father had just purchased. Unbeknownst to her at that time, she would spend the rest of her very long life there…. She eventually married George Weigel in 1918 after he returned from WWI…. Things went well until 1939, when George died unexpectedly. Augusta was left with a farm to run…. She was a very resourceful woman, though. She arranged a partnership with a local merchant, … secured a position with the state as a certified poultry and egg inspector ... [and] moonlighted as an instructor for the Northeastern Poultry Council. All in all, she was a busy woman ...

After reading the author's work, let students ask questions such as:

| Sample Questions from Students for a Local Writer |
|---|
| ♦ Do you tell the story to someone first, then write it down? |
| ♦ Is it really okay to write like you talk? |
| ♦ Why don't you pretend to interview people from the past? |
| ♦ How do you come up with an idea every week? |
| ♦ Where do you get your information? |
| ♦ Do you think all history should be written like this? |
| ♦ Do you like history? Did you like it in school? |
| ♦ Can you write another way or is this the only style you use? |
| ♦ What else do you write? |
| ♦ How did you learn to write this way? Can you teach us? |

The students learned to write about history in a conversational tone. Some of them might also get involved with the authors in identifying topics and doing research. The local connection and real-life writing piques students' interest and the inside scoop on how to write history so people like reading about it. You may find you have equally intriguing writers in your midst when you begin looking around. Take a moment and jot down some local writers or ways you might find them.

## Interview Students

What do your students read on their own? Comic books, magazines, internet sites? Find out what they read and why? What do they play with? Games, toys, puzzles? What is popular with each grade level? With boys, with girls? What do they care about? What issues are important to them? What do they want to know more about? How do they think they learn the best? What do they know the most about?

Interview students at each grade level to find out the answers to these questions, or have the upper grade students create and administer a survey to the school. Share the results with everyone and base your new classroom and library book orders on the topics of interest to students. Let parents know what students say they are interested in. Interviewing students lets them know you are listening and care about their interests and perspectives. You are modeling good listening and how to use what you learn in listening.

## Emphasize Learning as a Continuum

As you listen in on instruction and learning, parent-teacher conversations and student dialog, notice how they view learning. Is it a continuum? Or an on-off switch? Is it based on progress over time? Or a "see and do" model? The subtleties of how people communicate about learning lets you know if they are seeing learning as progress based on using strategies effectively. Talk to them about how they see learning, and let them know what you think.

## Expect Everyone to Speak Respectfully

"Sticks and stones may break my bones, but words can never hurt me." That childhood rhyme can't be further from the truth. But we always have a choice – to use our words to heal, to hear, to invite, to acknowledge, to build community, and to praise. There is no penalty for not knowing how, only for not caring, not being willing to learn, and not working together for the good of all. Every word counts—they add up, and they matter.

## Put Literacy Into the School Schedule

Because we see each other every day for 6 to 7 hours, the little things we do matter. The things we do and say every day accumulate in our community and magnify the effects: every day you put a greeting on an easel to students; every day you read aloud in the morning greeting; every day you spend 20 minutes reading for pleasure. Make these and other literacy activities routine in your school schedule.

This book suggests a theme for each month of the year and the plan book models how that might be done. Whole-school activities build excitement and connections among stu-

*Always read stuff that will make you look good if you die in the middle of it.*
—P. J. O'Rourke

dents. Add your own favorite routines from this book to each month to the calendar and you have a plan for the year you can share with teachers.

Books are suggested for each month that can be read by the whole school, or read aloud by you in classes, or used by the librarian. Use them to explore literacy themes in faculty meetings. Have your faculty plan by grade level to do something with the book and post the results in the halls. Reading a book as a school emphasizes the universal appeal of good literature and its importance as an expression of what it means to be human.

## Summary

Your students are with you, in your school, 40 or so weeks a year for about 6 to 7 hours per day. That gives you at least 1,600 hours to make a lasting impression about the importance of reading and literacy. Take advantage of this time to celebrate speaking and listening and encourage thoughtful, playful, and purposeful speaking and listening. There are those who will be authors as adults among you now. For today, everyone is a storyteller and a writer. Feature student and teacher authors in every way you can. Find writers from your community and help students learn from them. Developing connections with other writers, whether they are fellow students, teachers, or local professional writers, makes life-long impressions. The little things count a great deal. Five minutes here and 10 minutes there will add up to a lasting community of literacy that your students will take with them. Don't forget to share what you are reading. They are interested in you and your ideas and your thoughts too.

## Reflection

Think about whose voices are heard consistently—reading, telling stories, sharing ideas. Are student voices heard at least 70% of the time? If they are, then your culture is sending a clear message that their voices are important and that speaking and listening are integral to learning. If not, reflect on ways you can increase the volume and frequency of student voices.

# Conclusion

While there are many specific suggestions in this book, the key is in internalizing the question, "What does our culture say about what we believe about learning to read and write?" What are we doing and saying in all the every day small things we do, the celebrations we have, the way we organize our time and resources, and the language we use? If you look at the rules, roles, rituals, symbols, objects, language, and space of your school, what do you see? Look with fresh eyes at least every month and make a conscious decision to build a positive, powerful culture for learning to read and write.

- Every child can learn to read and write well.
- Language does not follow rules all the time.
- The basics of language can be defined and learned.
- Family literacy activities are at the center of children learning to read and reading to learn.
- The faculty that understands literacy development and uses data strengthens what they do with children.
- When students and teachers talk about strategies for reading and writing, everyone gets better faster.
- The stories we tell ourselves and others make our lives richer. Give children poetic license to tell the stories of their worlds.